Teachers and Families Working Together

FAMILY

TEACHERS

COMMUNITY

Teachers and Families Working Together

Deborah Diffily

Southern Methodist University

PEARSON

A and B

Boston ■ New York ■ San Francisco
Mexico City ■ Montreal ■ Toronto ■ London ■ Madrid ■ Munich ■ Paris
Hong Kong ■ Singapore ■ Tokyo ■ Cape Town ■ Sydney

This book is dedicated to Mike Hawkins, my son, who helped shape my thoughts and practices about working with families.

Series Editor: Traci Mueller

Editorial Assistant: Krista Price

Senior Marketing Manager: Elizabeth Fogarty

Editorial Production Administrator: Anna Socrates

Text Designer: Karen Mason

Editorial-Production Service: Susan McNally

Manufacturing Buyer: Andrew Turso

Composition and Prepress Buyer: Linda Cox

Cover Administrator: Kristina Mose-Libon

Electronic Composition: Modern Graphics

For related titles and support materials, visit our online catalog at www.ablongman.com.

Between the time Website information is gathered and then published, it is not unusual for some sites to have closed. Also, the transcription of URLs can result in unintended typographical errors. The publisher would appreciate notification where these errors occur so that they may be corrected in subsequent editions.

Library of Congress Cataloging-in-Publication Data

Diffily, Deborah.
   Teachers and families working together / by Deborah Diffily.
      p. cm.
   ISBN 0-205-37610-X
      1. Teachers—Professional relationships.   2. Education—Parent participation.
   I. Title.
   LB1175.D54 2003
   371.19′2—dc21

2003054145

Printed in the United States of America

10   9   8   7   6   5   4   3   08

Contents

Section II Barriers and Benefits

Section III Strategies to Communicate with and Involve Families

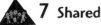

8 Other Ways to Communicate   99

9 Working through Cultural Differences between Teachers and Families   109

10 Working through Other Differences between Teachers and Families   132

Section IV Getting Started, Being Effective, and Moving Beyond Family Involvement

 11 Getting Started with Family Involvement and Moving into the Community   143

12 Being an Advocate for Young Children and Their Families   154

Appendix A Annotated Bibliography of Children's Books (Different Cultures and Family Types)   164

Foreword

When families are involved in children's education, the children do better in school. Abundant research now confirms the importance of family involvement, long recognized in the early childhood world and considerably less so in the world of schools. Although the challenges in building strong partnerships with families are not identical for schools and programs serving younger children, a great deal of commonality exists. Thus, there is much to be learned from the valuable experience that many early childhood educators have had in purposefully nurturing partnerships with parents. Deborah Diffily brings this experience, as well as familiarity with the school context, to the writing of *Teachers and Families Working Together*.

Early childhood teachers work very hard, and so do parents of young children. Families vary in all kinds of ways that affect their home life and their relationship to the school. Deborah's constant sensitivity to these realities informs all her work. She knows the myriad forms that families take and the fact that working with families can never be one-size-fits-all. With her knowledge of the challenges, Deborah is well aware that partnering with families is not just a matter of saying, "It's important, so do it!" In the present volume she demonstrates both this keen awareness of the obstacles and her abundant knowledge of how to overcome them.

This combination of sensitivity and practical know-how both were evident from the beginning of my own acquaintance with Dr. Diffily. I first met Deborah in 1994 at the National Association for the Education of Young Children (NAEYC) conference when she and her colleague Kathy Morrison sought me out to show me (in my role as NAEYC publications editor) a resource they and others in the Fort Worth Affiliate group had developed and were distributing as a fundraiser for the Affiliate. It was a collection of short, lively messages on topics that were important for families to know more about, including what goes on in good early childhood programs and why. Teachers were encouraged to use (and adapt) these pieces in newsletters and other communications with families.

Deborah and her associates recognized that, although early childhood teachers need and want to involve parents, they have limited time and resources for doing so. Give them a useful tool—in this case, a set of clear, well-written descriptions of what is behind early childhood practices and what families can do to contribute—and communication will improve! Out of this simple, powerful idea came the NAEYC publication, *Family Friendly Communication for Early Childhood Programs* (1996). Its immediate and continuing popularity testifies to the fact that the idea was right on target.

In *Teachers and Families Working Together*, Deborah again shows her commitment to both increasing teacher understanding and giving them practical strategies and tools. She ably summarizes the relevant research on their significance in children's educational lives and offers a wealth of proven ideas for working with families. Most distinctively, Deborah breathes life into the findings on key issues by introducing the voices of teachers, parents, children, and others speaking about those issues in their own experiences. We hear from a great variety of people about the home–school connection, or lack of it—what frustrates or disappoints them, what they struggle with, what they value, and how things look from where they sit.

Perhaps the most important of these voices for aspiring and practicing teachers to hear are those of family members. From their respective life circumstances, which vary widely, they talk about the difficulties they face with time, energy, and uncertainty about their role. They express how they value (or wish they could have) close connections with their children's educational lives. Certain to stay with readers long after most research details grow hazy, these voices do not merely embellish the text. They powerfully convey the whys and hows of involving families as partners in children's education.

With its clear presentation of the knowledge base, an abundance of useful strategies, and the authentic voices of families, teachers, and children, this book will make a lasting difference. It will move those who teach, I believe, to make partnering with families a high priority, and thus will multiply teachers' contribution to children's lives.

Carol Copple
National Association for the Education of Young Children
Publications Editor

Preface

There are many approaches one might take in writing a book about families and teachers working together.

To teacher educators who are reading this book, Parent Teacher Association (PTA) research (Henderson & Berla, 1995) indicates "one of the most significant challenges to conducting an effective program is the lack of instruction on parent and family involvement that educators and administrators receive in their professional training."

To administrators reading this book, PTA research (Henderson & Berla, 1995) shows that "when parents receive frequent and effective communication from the school or program, their involvement increases, their overall evaluation of education improves, and their attitudes toward the program are more positive."

To preservice teachers reading this book, PTA research (Henderson & Berla, 1995) asserts that "when parents are treated as partners and given relevant information by people with whom they are comfortable, parents put into practice the involvement strategies they already know are effective, but have been hesitant to contribute."

All of these voices were with me as I composed the first draft of the manuscript about teachers and families working together. Writing this book began a long time ago, probably during my first year of teaching. I had just finished a master's degree in early childhood education. My major professor, Margaret Puckett, used a recurring phrase: "Early childhood educators work with young children *and their families.*" Because of Dr. Puckett's teaching abilities, her scholarship, and her passion for young children, I accepted this recurring phrase as truth.

During my first year of teaching, I made it a point to remember some anecdote about each child to tell to parents who picked up their children after school, made a couple of telephone calls to mothers or fathers every afternoon to share some positive event with them, invited parents into the class anytime they found the time to drop in, wrote weekly letters to families so they would know what was going on in our class, and always included my home telephone number so families could call me if they had questions. Over time, I came to realize that other teachers at my school were not doing these things, and sometimes I found myself defending my practices. Other teachers were just not sure that getting so close to families was a good idea. Their opinions ranged from the belief that teachers should keep a professional distance to a concern that parents would try to take over if you let them get too close or spend too much time in the classroom.

The next year, I continued communicating with families in the same ways. But that year, my perspective on working with families changed somewhat. My conversations with families at the end of the day became more informative, phone calls were more detailed, and letters gave a better glimpse into our classroom. What changed that year was that my only son started school. In thinking about communicating with the families of my students, I found myself trying to do those things that I wished my son's teacher would do for me. I wanted to know as much as I could about his day, what he was doing, how he was getting along with the other children in his class, how he responded to things he was asked to do, what he chose during self-selected activity time, and generally what he was learning.

Margaret Puckett's teaching, and thinking about what I wished my son's teacher would do for me, continued to guide my decisions about working with families. Each year I modified the methods I used to communicate with families or added new methods to what I did. This book is the result of my work with a lot of families and my discussions with a lot of teachers about their experiences working with families.

This book is divided into four sections. The first section looks at family involvement from three perspectives: those of experts, families, and teachers. The second section examines the barriers to family involvement, from the perspectives of families and teachers, and the benefits of family involvement. Because I believe that when teachers realize how everyone benefits from families and teachers working together, the third section of this book details ways of working with families: written communication, shared time with families, other ways of communication, and working through differences between teachers and families. The fourth section is the final chapter of the book, which shares closing thoughts about working with families.

Please note that the pronoun "she" is used throughout this book when referring to teachers. This is not meant to ignore the fact that men do teach young children, but to reinforce the fact that the vast majority of early childhood educators are female. Most are also middle-class Caucasians. As we move into the twenty-first century, the field of early childhood education and the classrooms of young children need the contributions of more men, more people of color, and individuals from all cultural groups.

Acknowledgments

I appreciate all of the families who allowed me to teach their young children and who helped me learn what family involvement really meant. Their names are too numerous to itemize.

In writing this book, I am grateful to the early childhood educators and family members who allowed me to interview them and present their thoughts and perceptions in the following chapters. I especially appreciate Charlotte Sassman who served as my peer response partner for several drafts of each chapter. I would also like to thank the following reviewers: Eileen Donahue Brittain, Truman College; Dorothy Hewes, San Diego State University; Linda Medcaris, Texas A&M University; Peggy Pearl, Southwest Missouri State University; Maria Elena Reyes, University of Alaska, Fairbanks; and Terri Swim, University of Akron, provided helpful comments on the manuscript. Finally, I am thankful for such a responsive, supportive editor as I found in Traci Mueller.

1

FAMILY

TEACHERS

COMMUNITY

What the Experts Say about Family Involvement

Learning Objectives

The reader will learn and be able to discuss:

- A brief history of parental involvement in their child's education
- The positions of four national professional organizations about family involvement
- The view of four national organizations/agencies of family involvement

> Young children are integrally connected to their families.
> Programs cannot adequately meet the needs of children
> unless they also recognize the importance
> of the child's family and develop strategies
> to work effectively with all families.
>
> —National Association for the Education of Young Children, 1998

Promoting families' involvement in their children's education is supported by virtually all experts in the fields of early childhood education and school–family relations. There is general consensus that children simply do better in school when their parents are involved in their education; however, there is not a generally accepted definition of family involvement.

Family involvement covers a wide range of activities. A rather simple definition of family involvement relates to those things that families do at home to support their children's education, such as supervising homework. Some definitions also focus on what occurs at home, but are more proactive, suggesting such activities as reading together, monitoring television, establishing a daily family routine, monitoring out-of-school activities, talking with children, and communicating positive behaviors, values, and character traits (Ballen and Moles, 1994). The opposite end of the continuum defines family involvement as attending regular meetings with the classroom teacher and active participation in the life of the child's class (Diffily, 2001) or involvement in school reform efforts such as participating in the development of school improvement plans or serving on governance councils. A look at the historical perspective of family involvement indicates that the roots of early childhood education encouraged a more active sense of how families were involved in their children's educations.

The Historical Perspective on Parent Education/ Family Involvement

From prehistoric times, parents were their children's educators. All children's learning occurred within their families. Formal education received outside of the home environment did not emerge until some 4,000 years ago in Egypt. This education was for only a selected group of children from the most prosperous families. From the very beginnings of formal education, teachers were viewed as the experts. When families could access formal education for their children, they relinquished the role of teacher, turning this over to education experts. The separation of the roles of teacher and parent continued for centuries.

Not until the late nineteenth century did the concept of teachers and parents working together to educate children emerge (Berger, 1991). Organizations formed to study children and promote what was best for them. These organizations became a driving force in fostering parent education programs. Within a few years, the federal government also became a major factor in educating parents.

Several women's organizations were formed in the 1880s and 1890s. Each of them included the study of children in their educational programs. These organizations included the American Association of University Women (AAUW), the Congress of Parents and Teachers, which was called the PTA, and the National Association of Colored Women. The Child Study Association of America was also founded during this time period.

The federal government assumed a leadership role in educating parents in the early twentieth century. In 1909, the first White House Conference on the Care of Dependent Children was held. Three years later, the Children's Bureau was established to implement some of the recommendations made during the White House Conference. By 1914, federal legislation provided 2,000 county home demonstration agents, charging them with the job of educating parents.

Parent education flourished throughout the twentieth century. During the decade of the 1920s, more families became involved in organized programs. The Child Study Association of America, founded in 1888, grew from 56 parent groups in 1926 to 135 in 1927 (Whipple, 1929). Membership in Parent/Teacher Associations swelled from 190,000 in 1920 to almost 1,500,000 in 1930 (Schlossman, 1976). In the 1930s, when the economic depression redirected many families' attention from their children to simple survival, the federal government continued its commitment to parent education. Many of the agencies established to support the economy also included programs to support children and their families. The Works Progress Administration (WPA) sponsored a program to help families learn about managing the home. The Federal Emergency Relief Administration (FERA) provided salaries for unemployed teachers to organize nursery schools for young children and to work with parents of those children. In the 1940s, when families became consumed with the war effort, parent education programs continued. Child care was provided by government entities and corporations so that parents could work.

The federal government's role in parent education continued in the 1960s, especially in programs established to fight the "war on poverty." This role was very clear in the formation of the Head Start program, which was established to educate preschool children from low-income homes. Parent involvement was one of the four primary components of all Head Start programs. Research of Head Start, and other educational programs with a strong parent involvement component, began to be reported in the 1970s and 1980s. This research found that stronger involvement of families in their children's educations resulted in more success for the children in school (Powell, 1989).

Beginning in the 1980s, parent education, parent participation, and parent involvement were promoted by a wide variety of professional organizations and other national organizations and agencies. These included the National Association for the Education of Young Children, the Association for Childhood Education International, the International Reading Association, the Council for Exceptional Children, the National Association of State Boards of Education, and the United States Department of Education. These organizations continue to promote families' involvement in their children's education.

The Positions of Professional Organizations

Just as professional organizations began the parent education movement in the late nineteenth century, professional organizations lead current efforts in family involvement and parent education.

The National Association for the Education of Young Children

The National Association for the Education of Young Children (NAEYC) strongly advocates family involvement and the role of teachers in encouraging this involvement. NAEYC, a professional organization for early childhood professionals representing more than 125,000 members, takes the lead in developing and publishing position statements about early childhood education in general and specifically addresses many issues related to early childhood. In its 1997 revised edition of *Developmentally Appropriate Practice in Early Childhood Programs*, five interrelated dimensions of early childhood practice are presented as guidelines for making decisions about developmentally appropriate practice. These five dimensions are:

1. Creating a caring community of learners
2. Teaching to enhance development and learning
3. Constructing appropriate curriculum
4. Assessing children's learning and development
5. Establishing reciprocal relationships with families (Bredekamp and Copple, 1997)

Placing relationships with families as one of the five guidelines for developmentally appropriate practice clearly demonstrates how strongly NAEYC values the work of early childhood educators with families. Bredekamp and Copple (1997) define the type of relationship that quality early childhood educators develop with the families of their students. They go on to describe several teacher behaviors that help establish and maintain good relationships with family members. The following eight points are found in Part I of *Developmentally Appropriate Practices in Early Childhood Programs* (Bredekamp and Copple, 1997):

A. *Reciprocal relationships between teachers and families require mutual respect, cooperation, shared responsibility, and negotiation of conflicts toward achievement of shared goals.*

B. *Early childhood teachers work in collaborative partnerships with families, establishing and maintaining regular, frequent two-way communication with children's parents.*

C. *Parents are welcome in the program and participate in decisions about their children's care and education. Parents observe and participate and serve in decision-making roles in the program.*

D. *Teachers acknowledge parents' choices and goals for children and respond with sensitivity and respect to parents' preferences and concerns without abdicating professional responsibility to children.*

E. *Teachers and parents share their knowledge of the child and understanding of children's development and learning as part of day-to-day communication and planned conferences. Teachers support families in ways that maximally promote family decision-making capabilities and competence.*

F. *To ensure more accurate and complete information, the program involves families in assessing and planning for individual children.*

G. *The program links families in assessing and planning for individual children.*

H. *Teachers, parents, programs, social service and health agencies, and consultants who may have educational responsibility for the child at different times should, with family participation, share developmental information about children as they pass from one level or program to another.* (p. 22)

Clearly, NAEYC takes a strong stand on the need to involve families in their children's education and places responsibility on teachers and families to work together in collaboration. These guidelines do, however, imply that teachers have primary responsibility for keeping families informed and encouraging families to become involved at school and with teachers.

NAEYC confirms its stance on the importance of teacher/family relationships and supports the work of teachers through the resources it provides for early childhood educators. In the past five years, more than seventy-five articles related to families

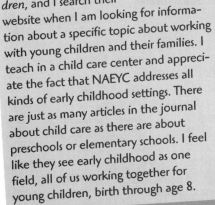

VOICES *of Teachers*

I am a member of NAEYC. I look forward to reading the journal, *Young Children*, and I search their website when I am looking for information about a specific topic about working with young children and their families. I teach in a child care center and appreciate the fact that NAEYC addresses all kinds of early childhood settings. There are just as many articles in the journal about child care as there are about preschools or elementary schools. I feel like they see early childhood as one field, all of us working together for young children, birth through age 8.

have appeared in NAEYC's journal, *Young Children*. Written by researchers, college professors, and expert practitioners, the articles range from how to hold effective conferences with families to helping families better understand developmentally appropriate practices. For a partial listing of these articles, see Box 1.1.

National Parent-Teacher Association

The Parent-Teacher Association (PTA) is another national organization that takes a strong position about parent involvement. The PTA's position is that family involvement in the schools has a profound influence on children's academic success. The PTA also contends that family involvement offers comprehensive benefits for all parties involved: the students, the families, the teachers, and the schools.

BOX 1.1 | *Young Children's Articles Related to Working with Families*

Buell, M. J., Hallam, R.A., & Beck, H. L. (2001). Early Head Start and child care partnerships: Working together to serve infants, toddlers, and their families. *Young Children, 56,* 7–12.

Coleman, M. (1997). Families and schools: In search of common ground. *Young Children, 52,* 14–21.

Egley, E. H., & Egley, R. J. (2000). Teaching principals, parents, and colleagues about developmentally appropriate practice. *Young Children, 55,* 48–51.

Eldridge, D. (2001). Parent involvement: It's worth the effort. *Young Children, 56,* 65–69.

File, N. (2001). Family-professional partnerships: Practice that matches philosophy. *Young Children, 56,* 70–74.

Gorter-Reu, M. S., & Anderson, J. M. (1998). Home kits, home visits, and more! *Young Children, 53,* 71–74.

Hurt, J. A. (2000). Create a parent place: Make the invitation for family involvement real. *Young Children, 55,* 88–92.

Kaufman, H. O. (2001). Skills for working with all families. *Young Children, 56,* 81–83.

Koch, P. K., & McDonough, M. (1999). Improving parent-teacher conferences through collab-

orative conversations. *Young Children, 54,* 11–15.

Manning, D., & Schindler, P. J. (1997). Communicating with parents when their children have difficulties. *Young Children, 52,* 27–33.

McBride, S. L. (1999). Family-centered practices, research in review. *Young Children, 54,* 62–68.

Okagaki, L., & Diamond, K. E. (2000). Responding to cultural and linguistic differences in the beliefs and practices of families with young children. *Young Children, 55,* 74–80.

Sturm, C. (1997). Creating parent-teacher dialogue: Intercultural communication in child care. *Young Children, 52,* 34–38.

Turbiville, V. P., Umbarger, G. T., & Guthrie, A. C. (2000). Fathers' involvement in programs for young children. *Young Children, 55,* 74–79.

Walker-Dalhouse, D., & Dalhouse, A. D. (2001). Parent-school relations: Communicating more effectively with African American parents. *Young Children, 56,* 75–80.

Webb, N. C. (1997). Working with parents from cradle to preschool: A university collaborates with an urban public school. *Young Children, 52,* 15–19.

The National PTA created standards for parent/family involvement programs. These standards are based on the work of Anne Henderson and Nancy Berla, who conducted extensive research on family involvement and authored three documents that summarize their research and the research of others. These documents are *The Evidence Grows* (1981), *The Evidence Continues to Grow* (1987), and *A New Generation of Evidence: The Family Is Critical to Student Achievement* (1995). All three publications discuss the positive results of parents and other caretaking family members becoming active participants in children's education. On their website, the National PTA summarizes the eighty-five research studies cited in the three documents by listing the following eleven research findings:

- ☑ When parents are involved, students achieve more, regardless of socioeconomic status, ethnic/racial background, or the parents' education level.
- ☑ The more extensive the parent involvement, the higher the student achievement.
- ☑ When parents are involved in their children's education, those students have higher grades and test scores, better attendance, and complete homework more consistently.
- ☑ When parents are involved, students exhibit more positive attitudes and behavior.
- ☑ Students whose parents are involved in their lives have higher graduation rates and greater enrollment rates in post-secondary education.
- ☑ Educators hold higher expectations of students whose parents collaborate with the teacher.
- ☑ In programs that are designed to involve parents in full partnerships, achievement for disadvantaged students improves, and can reach levels that are standard for middle-class students. In addition, the students who are farthest behind make the greatest gains.
- ☑ Students from diverse cultural backgrounds tend to do better when parents and professionals collaborate to bridge the gap between the culture at home and the learning institution.
- ☑ Student behaviors such as alcohol use, violence, and antisocial behavior decrease as parent involvement increases.
- ☑ Students are more likely to fall behind in academic performance if their parents do not participate in school events, develop a working relationship with their child's educators, or keep up with what is happening in their child's school.
- ☑ The benefits of involving parents are not confined to the early years; there are significant gains at all ages and grade levels.
- ☑ The most accurate predictor of a student's achievement in school is not income or social status, but the extent to which that student's family is able to (1) create a home environment that encourages learning; (2) communicate high, yet reasonable, expectations for their children's achievement and future careers; and (3) become involved in their children's education at school and in the community (National PTA, 2002).

VOICES *of Families*

PTA was the way I learned just how important it was for me to be involved in my child's education. I don't remember my parents being involved in my education at all. They came to teacher conferences, but that was it. Another mother called and asked me to the first PTA meeting when my son was in kindergarten. It felt like everyone who talked that day was talking to me. I needed to talk to my child about what he did at school. I needed to visit the class and see exactly how he was learning. I needed to support the teacher. PTA changed how I saw my role as a parent.

The National PTA believes so strongly in the benefits of family involvement in the schools that it makes the following summary statement on its website:

> After 30 years, research has proven beyond dispute the positive connection between parent involvement and student success. Effectively engaging parents and families in the education of their children has the potential to be far more transformational than any other type of education reform (National PTA, 2002).

The National PTA offers support for parents, teachers, and administrators who want to work on creating strong family involvement programs. As a framework for these programs, the National PTA created six standards.

Standard I: Communicating Communication between home and school is regular, two-way, and meaningful.

Standard II: Parenting Parenting skills are promoted and supported.

Standard III: Student Learning Parents play an integral role in assisting student learning.

Standard IV: Volunteering Parents are welcome in the school, and their support and assistance are sought.

Standard V: School Decision Making and Advocacy Parents are full partners in the decisions that affect children and families.

Standard VI: Collaborating with Community Community resources are used to strengthen schools, families, and student learning.

Quality indicators are available to explain each standard more clearly. The indicators identify the important elements of each standard and offer sample applications to show how some programs meet each standard.

National Black Child Development Institute

Established in 1970, the National Black Child Development Institute's (NBCDI) mission is to improve and protect the quality of life of African American children and their families. The organization believes that everyone in the community must play a role in creating equity and access for all African American children, but acknowledges the important role of parents in the lives of their children.

NBCDI has a family education program called Parents Empowerment Program. It was developed by and for inner-city African American families, but it has been used with families of all ethnicities. This program helps parents learn to:

- ☑ Express and demonstrate knowledge of child development and parenting skills
- ☑ Stimulate their child's growth and development appropriately
- ☑ Increase their knowledge of community resources and how to access them
- ☑ Develop confidence and positive self-esteem (www.nbcdi.org/pep.htm)

In the fall of 2002, NBCDI launched the African American Parents' Program. This program was developed to disseminate information and share resources with families so that they can provide their children with a sense of comfort and safety in times of violence or other events that provoke fear in children. This program was developed in the aftermath of September 11, 2001, but is not limited to terrorism. The African American Parents' Program helps parents understand how much influence they have over a child's coping skills and in giving them tools to hold age-appropriate conversations about things that frighten them.

National Education Association

The National Education Association (NEA) describes itself as the oldest and largest organization committed to public education, making public education available to all students, and supporting causes related to public education. NEA was founded in 1857 in Philadelphia. It has almost 3 million members who work at all levels of education from preschool through university graduate school.

NEA recognizes parents as the child's first—and perhaps the most important—teacher. It acknowledges the importance of family involvement in children's success at school. NEA has affiliates in all fifty states and more than 13,000 communities across the nation.

NEA offers resources to support families' work with their own children. Among the printed resources are twelve books written for teachers to help them build partnerships with families. Among the online resources for parents related to their children's education are articles about promoting reading, building partnerships between families and teachers, and specific strategies for supporting children's academic learning.

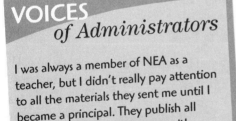

VOICES *of Administrators*

I was always a member of NEA as a teacher, but I didn't really pay attention to all the materials they sent me until I became a principal. They publish all kinds of great materials to use with teachers to help them involve family members, and they publish quality materials for parents to help them understand their role in their children's educations. I depend on organizations like NEA for books, pamphlets, and brochures to share with others.

The Views of National Organizations and Agencies

Center on School, Family, and Community Partnerships

The Center on School, Family, and Community Partnerships was founded on the simple belief that children will be more successful in school when schools, families, and communities work together for the benefit of students. The mission of the Center is to conduct and disseminate research, development, and policy analyses that produce new and useful knowledge and practices that help families, educators, and members of communities work together to improve schools, strengthen families, and enhance student learning and development.

Joyce Epstein is a professor of Sociology at Johns Hopkins University, and the Director of the Center on School, Family, and Community Partnerships. Epstein has published prolifically (Brandt, 1989). She has over one hundred publications on the effects of school, classroom, family, and peer environments on student learning and development, with many focusing on school and family connections. Through her research, Epstein developed a categorization of the types of parent involvement (Epstein, 2001).

1. *Parenting* Help all families establish home environments to support children as students.
2. *Communicating* Design effective forms of school-to-home and home-to-school communications about school programs and children's progress.
3. *Volunteering* Recruit and organize parent help and support.
4. *Learning at Home* Provide information and ideas to families about how to help students at home with homework and other curriculum-related activities, decisions, and planning.
5. *Decision Making* Include parents in school decisions, developing parent leaders and representatives.
6. *Collaborating with Community* Identify and integrate resources and services from the community to strengthen school programs, family practices, and student learning and development.

National Coalition for Parent Involvement in Education

The National Coalition for Parent Involvement in Education was established in 1980 with the mission to advocate the involvement of parents and families in their children's education, and to foster relationships between home, school, and community to enhance the education of all our nation's young people. As an active coalition, this organization attempts to

 Serve as a visible representative for strong parent and family involvement initiatives at the national level

☑ Conduct activities that involve the coalition's member organizations and their affiliates and constituencies in efforts to increase family involvement

☑ Provide resources and legislative information that can help member organizations promote parent and family involvement

This Coalition also acts as a clearinghouse for publications related to families and schools, with such varied resources as *Grandparents Raising Their Grandchildren: What to Consider and Where to Find Help*, published by the American Association of Retired Persons; *Beyond the Bake Sale: An Educator's Guide to Working With Families*, published by the Center for Law and Education; and *Involving Parents in Schools*, published by the National Association of Elementary School Principals. These resources are organized by audience (parents, teachers, communities), by the organization that published the original work, or by subject (after-school programs, at-risk students, child care, community education, community partnerships, diversity, early childhood education, elementary education, higher education, high school education, information and referral, literacy, middle school education, parent education, parent leadership, promising practices for education, promising practices for parent involvement, public policy, and research).

United States Department of Education

PARTNERSHIP FOR FAMILY INVOLVEMENT IN EDUCATION   Family involvement is such a crucial component of effective education that the Department of Education established a special program focused on family involvement. The Partnership for Family Involvement in Education was formed in September of 1994. Recognizing that the extent of a family's involvement in their children's learning is often influenced by work schedules and time constraints, this Partnership includes businesses, community, and religious organizations, as well as families and schools in their plans to support parent involvement in education. To encourage this broad level of support from multiple sources, the Department of Education administers the Partnership and offers resources, ideas, funding, and conferences relevant to family involvement in education. Different plans—Employers for Learning, Community Organizations, Religious Groups, and Family-School Partnerships—encourage commitment to increasing family participation in children's learning through a variety of activities and efforts. Some of these include student- and family-friendly policies at the workplace, before- and after-school programs, tutoring and mentoring initiatives, and donations of facilities and technologies.

The U.S. Department of Education assumes a primary role in the Partnership. It provides a network of support for the companies and organizations around the country working to make education a community concern. The Department of Education encourages partners to connect with each other, collaborate, combine resources, and share ideas and best practices. The Department of Education also attempts to keep partners informed of current educational issues and trends and to provide resources and publications to improve local and state programs. These resources can be found on the Partnership for Family Involvement in Education's website.

THE NATIONAL INSTITUTE ON EARLY CHILDHOOD DEVELOPMENT AND EDUCATION   The National Institute on Early Childhood Development and Education is also housed in the federal Department of Education, in the Office of Educational Research and Improvement. This program was created to conduct research, develop programs, and disseminate information about what they refer to as the three Rs of early childhood education: relationships, resilience, and readiness. In each of these three areas, families are considered crucial. Even though the focus of the National Institute on Early Childhood Development and Education is early childhood education and not families, the importance of families during the early childhood years leads much discussion and support of family involvement by this agency.

The National Institute on Early Childhood Development and Education offers resources to families and early childhood educators for their collaboration through the Early Childhood Digests with such topics as helping parents communicate better with schools, family involvement in early childhood programs, and families and teachers as partners. Research projects and program initiatives funded through the National Institute on Early Childhood Development and Education can be found on the Institute's website under its Directory. These studies and initiatives are funded through 2003, and their results will be published on the Institute's website.

 Summary

Several national organizations and agencies related to schools and children recognize the benefits of family involvement on children's academic success. They provide rationales for and resources to support family involvement.

 **Reflections**

1. Consider the stances about family involvement taken by different organizations and individuals. Which most closely reflects your current beliefs about working with families? Why?
2. Consider the information about family involvement offered by each organization and agency. Which appears to be the most helpful to individual teachers trying to encourage family involvement? Why?

 **Field Experiences**

1. Choose two articles from Box 1.1, get copies, and read them. Interview two teachers and two parents about their feelings about family involvement. Compare and contrast teachers'/families' thoughts and feelings to the information you read in the journal articles.
2. Consider how teachers'/families' thoughts and feelings support or extend ideas about family involvement presented by the journal articles or the organizations or agencies discussed in this chapter.

 **Other Activities**

1. Start a file for journal articles about family involvement. Copy articles that are particularly informative or interesting.

2. Select one of the child-family-related organizations that was established near the end of the nineteenth century or the beginning of the twentieth century. Research the reasons the organization was founded and some of its early work designed to benefit children and their families. Share that research with the class.
3. Locate the websites for the organizations and agencies discussed in this chapter and review the information on each website. Create files on each organization and agency for future reference.
4. Locate websites for local school districts. Search the sites for references to the importance of family involvement.

Further Readings

Martin, E. J., & Hagan-Burke, S. (2002). Establishing a home-school connection: Strengthening the partnership between families and schools. *Preventing School Failure, 46*, 62–66.

    This article describes seven steps that enhance communication between families and teachers.

Zigler, E., & Muenchow, S. (1994). *Head Start: The inside story of American's most successful education.* New York: Basic Books.

    Using Zigler's personal experiences as a founder of Head Start and Muenshow's historical and field research, this book details the story of Head Start, from its beginnings in the 1960s through its current operation.

Websites to Explore

- National Association for the Education of Young Children
  1509 16th Street, NW
  Washington, DC 20019
  Phone: 800-424-2460
  Fax: 202-328-1846
  http://www.naeyc.org/

- National Black Child Development Institute
  1101 15th Street N.W., Suite 900
  Washington, DC 20005
  202-833 2220
  Fax: 202-833-8222
  http://www.nbcdi.org

- National Coalition for Parent Involvement in Education
  3929 Old Lee Highway, Suite 91-A
  Fairfax, VA 22030-2401
  Voice: 703-359-8973
  Fax: 703-359-0972
  http://www.ncpie.org/

- National Education Association
  1201 16th Street, N.W.
  Washington, DC 20036-3290
  202-833-4000
  http://www.nea.org

- The National Institute on Early Childhood Development and Education
  Office of Educational Research and Improvement
  U.S. Department of Education
  555 New Jersey Ave, NW
  Washington, DC 20208
  Phone: 202-219-1935
  http://www.ed.gov/offices/OERI/ECI/

- National Parent-Teacher Association
  330 N. Wabash Avenue
  Suite 2100
  Chicago, IL 60611
  Phone: 312-670-6782
  Toll-Free: 800-307-4PTA (4782)
  Fax: 312-670-6783
  http://www.pta.org/index.asp

- The Partnership for Family Involvement in Education
  U.S. Department of Education
  400 Maryland Avenue, SW
  Washington, DC 20202-8173
  http://pfie.ed.gov/

2

FAMILY

TEACHERS

COMMUNITY

What Families Say about Family Involvement

Learning Objectives

The reader will learn and be able to discuss:

- Different family configurations
- Some unique needs of the different family configurations
- How early childhood educators can support the needs of different families

Families care about their children's success,
but most parents need more and better information
from schools and communities
to become and remain
productively involved in their child's education.

—Joyce Epstein, 2001

When asked about the issue, most families indicate that they think their involvment in their children's education benefits the child. However, as questioning continues, the positive attitude about family involvement becomes more tentative, especially when asked about their personal involvement in their child's school. Some parents indicate that they are very active in their child's class, and a few truly are. A few parents spend an hour or two every week in their child's classroom, supporting instruction by reading or listening to children or assisting in an activity where children are working in small groups. A few more parents are actually supportive of the child's school by volunteering to work in the office, in the library, or at parent–teacher association sponsored events. In reality, the percentage of family members who are active at their child's school is relatively low.

Families who spend time in their child's classroom and attend evening or weekend meetings say that they started this involvement because of a specific request from a teacher. Parents indicate that they are much more likely to become involved in schools when it seems to them that the school is specifically working to get them involved. When parents have a positive experience the first time they attend an event or volunteer at school, they are likely to repeat those experiences. On the other hand, when families have a negative experience at school during their first steps of becoming involved, they may never volunteer again. The vast majority of these families will return only with repeated invitations and personal encouragement from teachers. Even for families who are involved at school, a single negative experience may decrease the family's interest in staying involved.

Many parents say that when a teacher contacts them, it is usually because of a problem with their child. These families frequently say that if the teacher is going to deliver only bad news, they are not going to go out of their way to spend time in their child's class or even talk to the teacher (Rimm-Kaufman and Pianta, 1999).

Most parents are not involved at the class level or the school level. For a variety of reasons, many parents do not feel comfortable about becoming actively involved in the classroom. These reasons are discussed in detail in Chapter 4.

It is difficult to describe today's families. Children are now living in a greater variety of family configurations than in previous generations, and families need more support than in previous generations. Past generations relied on extended family members to help with child-rearing advice and support. That has changed substantially. "An increasing number of families do not stay in one place long enough to develop the intricate neighborhood and community connections that were once the mainstay of mutual support" (Weissbourd, 1987, p. 46). With the general population more mobile than ever before, families with young children are more likely to live away from their parents or other close relatives. For this reason, many families look to teachers to provide the support that previous generations received from their own families.

Family Types

Many family configurations in the twenty-first century will be discussed in this chapter. They are:

- ☑ "Traditional" Families
- ☑ Two-Career Families
- ☑ Blended Families
- ☑ Single-Parent Families
- ☑ Gay and Lesbian Families
- ☑ Families Raising Grandchildren
- ☑ Families with Adopted Children
- ☑ Families with Foster Children
- ☑ Families with Children with Special Needs
- ☑ Homeless Families

All families within each configuration share some aspects of lifestyle. All families deal with the day-to-day physical needs of children: housing, food, clothing. Most families have to consider the cost and quality of child care for at least part of the week. Most families think about helping their children develop qualities they consider important for successful adults. Virtually all families want what is best for their children.

At the same time, within each configuration, families also differ widely in their needs, their beliefs, and their values. Each family type is described briefly in the following sections, and a few statistics are offered. For "the voices" shared in each section below, one person from each family configuration was interviewed. Their responses to open-ended questions such as "Tell me a little about your role in your family" and "How do you view your role in your child's education" are offered as examples of family beliefs—with the understanding that the opinions of the individuals interviewed are not representative of everyone within that family type.

"Traditional" Families

Many people think of the traditional family as a working father, a stay-at-home mother, and two or three children. Today these families are often referred to as the Cleaver family, referring to the 1950s television program, *Leave It to Beaver*. This family type is less common than most believe. In the mid-1990s, only 7% of mothers in a two-parent household stayed home with children while the father went to work (Fuller, 1993).

The definition of traditional family is moving toward "a married mother and father living with their biological children." This type of family is increasing. These families represented 51% (in 1991) to 56% (in 1996) of 71.5 million children (Fields, 2001). Fewer African American children live in this traditional nuclear family configuration (26%) than do children in other racial/ethnic groups; 65% of white children, 58% of Asian and Pacific Islander children, and 48% of Hispanic children live in nuclear families (Fields, 2001).

Two-Career Families

More than 70% of married people with children both work outside the home (Fields, 2001). Juggling the responsibilities of two careers affects family time and the way many of these parents interact with their children. Virtually all families can benefit from a workshop about communicating with children. This may be particularly appropriate for two-career families. Limited time with children requires effective communication and conflict resolution (PTA, 2002).

VOICES *of Families*

I'm a stay-at-home mom. My husband works about sixty hours a week, so most of the responsibilities of the house and the children fall to me. It may not be an exciting life, but I think that what I am doing for my family is important. Both of my children are in school, so I pretty much have from 8:30 to 2:30 to do housework and run errands and those kinds of chores. Other than that, my children are pretty much my life. I want to be the one who takes them to school in the morning and picks them up in the afternoon. My husband and I made this decision together. He would work. I would stay home. In our neighborhood I am the only mother who does not work. I love being there for my children, but there is one thing about being a stay-at-home mom that bothers me a lot. Everyone thinks since I don't "work" that I won't mind doing favors for them—you know, things like waiting for repairmen or having things delivered to my house.

About my children's educations, I want to be involved. My mom was involved in school when I was in elementary school. I always thought that was so great that my mom was at my school a lot. Now I try to do that for my children. I go to all of the meetings called by my children's teachers, and make most of the PTA meetings. I volunteer in both children's classes. I spend an hour a week in each classroom, working with small groups of children on reading and writing. That, I enjoy doing. I feel like I am really helping the teacher and the children.

But the same sort of thing happens at school that happens in the neighborhood. Working parents seem to feel I should do more than they do. Whenever it's time to pick the room mother, everyone looks at me. I don't mind doing my share, but it is not fair that other parents just assume I have more time than they do. I want to be involved in my children's school. I just don't want everyone assuming that I'll do whatever they do not want to do (personal communication, Beth Saladino, 5 May 2002).

Blended Families

Of all children under the age of eighteen, 17% live in blended families. This number represents 11.8 million children. Blended families occur in two primary ways: living with half-siblings or living with a stepparent. Almost 8 million children live in families where a half-sibling is present in the home. This represents 11% of all children and 66% of all children living in blended families. Approximately 2.3 million children live with a stepparent. This represents 3% of all children and 20% of all children living in blended families. The remaining 14% of children who lived in blended families live in other configurations of stepsiblings only; stepparent and stepsibling; or stepparent, stepsibling, and half-sibling (Fields, 2001).

VOICES *of Families*

I'm the mother of one first-grade son. My husband and I both work, and we share all the things you have to do to raise a child and maintain a house. Well, I think I do a lot more than my husband does. But I think my role in my family is to keep things going. I make sure that there is food in the house, and I am the one that cooks. I make sure that we all have clean clothes to wear, and that the house is reasonably clean. I juggle schedules of where we are all supposed to be for soccer practices and games and play dates and things like that. I honestly don't know how people with more than one child manage. My husband and I are fortunate in that both our jobs have some flexibility for those times when our son is sick or has half-days at school.

Since our son is only in first grade, he does not have a lot of homework that we have to super-

vise. His teacher asks that we listen to him read every night and that we read to him. She sends home books, which is a really good thing 'cause I wouldn't know the right books he should be reading and he always likes it when we read books that are popular in his class. This is something that my husband and I both do. We take turns, kind of every other night, and that takes about 30 minutes after I get my son ready for bed. Other than helping him with his homework, there is not a lot more that we do about his education. His teacher did ask for parent volunteers at the beginning of the year, but I got the feeling she wanted people to do the same thing the same time every week. My job is flexible, but not that flexible. I can't be at school every week, but if you count going to meetings, I do go to PTA meetings. Does that count? (personal communication, Samantha Castillo, 22 May 2002).

Blended families experience the same challenges as all families, but there are additional issues, especially for the first few months after the two families begin living together. Children have concerns about what to call the stepparent and why this new person can tell them what to do when, according to the child, this person is not their real dad (or mom). Change is not particularly easy for young children, and getting a new parent is a rather considerable change. Perhaps even more disconcerting for children of a blended family is leaving their house and moving into the house of the stepparent. Children experiencing this level of change in their lives need additional emotional support as they adjust to their new living arrangements.

Just as children need the support of their teacher, the adult family members may also turn to the teacher for support and understanding. Early childhood educators are careful to be good listeners without overstepping professional boundaries and giving specific advice. Generic advice and the recommendation to consider

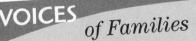

VOICES of Families

I am married to a woman with three children and I have two children from a previous marriage, so sometimes we are a family of five, and every other weekend we are a family of seven. I see my role in the family as provider and guider. I work longer hours than I would like because I want all my children to have what they need. I try to be at home on the weekends that my children are with us, but that doesn't always work out.

I would like to be able to say that my wife and I are active at school. I remember when my mom was, well, she was like the mom-in-charge-of-parties when I was in third grade. I really liked that she came to the class parties and brought cool food and favors. All the other children would say what a great mom she was, and I liked that. Unfortunately, with five children and their schedules and our jobs, my wife's and mine, we just don't have the kind of time my mother had. We can't be involved like my mother was (personal communication, John Crites, 24 May 2002).

family counseling is acceptable. Teachers can encourage blended families to build strong bonds among themselves. Suggestions include: developing new skills in making decisions as a family; fostering and strengthening new relationships between parents, stepparent and stepchild, and stepsiblings; supporting one another; and maintaining and nurturing original parent–child relationships (American Academy of Child and Adolescent Psychiatry, 1999b).

Single-Parent Families

According to U.S. Census statistics, 18.2 million children are living with only one unmarried parent (Fields, 2001). The percentage of single-parent families doubled between 1970 and 1990, from 6 to 12% of all families. Since 1990 it has only increased two percentage points (Cable News Network, 1998). Divorce is a large factor in the increase in single-parent families. However, the divorce rate appears to be slowing, with 4.1 divorces per 1,000 people in 1995, down from 4.7 in 1990 and 5.0 in 1985 (Cable News Network, 1998).

In 1997, single-parent families accounted for 64.4% of African American families with young children, 36.1% among Hispanics, and 26.3% of whites. The proportion of single mothers to single fathers was 83% versus 17% (Cable News Network, 1998).

Single parents face all the same problems of child-rearing that traditional families do; however, they face these problems without the support of a spouse. Teachers are not in the position of actually providing this support, but can recommend support groups such as Parents Without Partners or similar resources.

Gay and Lesbian Families

All too often, people think of gay and lesbian families as a very small number of families living in the large urban communities. The 2000 United States Census Bureau figures contradict this general belief. In 2000, 601,209 gay and lesbian families (304,148 gay male families and 297,061 lesbian families) lived in 99.3% of all

VOICES *of Families*

I am raising three children all by myself. My husband left us a year ago. My family lives 1,000 miles away. It's just me, with an eleven-year-old, a seven-year-old, and a three-year-old. This means every morning I have to drop kids off at the middle school, the elementary school, and the child care center, and then get myself to work. I work all day, so my older two have to take care of themselves until I get off work, pick up the baby, and make it home. Then it's time to make dinner, wash clothes, clean the house, and try to spend some time with my kids. Every day, it is the same. Too much to do and not enough time to do it in. But, you know, even though it's not an easy life, it's better for my kids. Before he left, my husband and I used to fight a lot. The tension in the house was so thick, you could cut it with a knife. That wasn't good for the kids. I may be tired now, but I focus on my kids more now than I did then.

How do I see my role in my children's education? That's not an easy question. There are almost two different answers. I think when my older two were little, I was good at teaching them stuff like their colors, and their numbers, and their letters. They both knew all that kind of thing before they went to kindergarten. When they went to school, I did what the teacher asked parents to do, like read with them, play games with them, that kind of thing. But that was a few years ago. Now that it is just me, I don't have the time to teach the youngest one like I did the others, and I am not as good at helping with homework as I was when they were little, especially the oldest. He is starting to learn things in middle school that I don't even remember studying. I can't help him with math or science, not even grammar. So, at one time, I think I was an important part of my children's education, and now, I don't think I am (personal communication, Leslie Johnson, 19 April 2002).

United States counties (U.S. Census Bureau, 2001). These numbers represent a dramatic increase over 1990 census statistics. In 1990, the U.S. Census Bureau reported 145,130 gay and lesbian families—81,343 male and 63,787 female—living in 52% of all counties. The 2000 numbers represent a 314% increase in gay and lesbian families in one decade, and the Human Rights Campaign (the largest national lesbian and gay political organization) estimates that the 2000 U.S. Census count of gay and lesbian families could be undercounted by as much as 62%. This contention is supported by a 2002 survey conducted by Witeck-Combs Communications, a gay marketing company. This survey indicates that more than 3 million children live with gay and lesbian parents in the United States, and Witeck-Combs predicts that by 2004 there will be 3.4 million children in gay homes (www.proudparenting.com).

Although research (Stacey and Biblarz, 2001) indicates that the sexual orientation of a parent is irrelevant to a child's social, emotional, and cognitive develop-

VOICES *of Families*

I am just about the same as other mothers. Just because my life partner is another woman doesn't make my role as a mother any different. I am the one of us that keeps up with the logistics of keeping the family organized. I plan the meals, shop for groceries, and cook meals. We both work, so we hire help for cleaning the house, laundry, and those kinds of things. We've had our daughter in child care since she was six months old. Because of that, evenings and weekends are family time. The three of us spend that time together. We take that time seriously and specifically plan activities that are both educational and fun. Music is a big part of our lives. We both play musical instruments, so we often play in the evenings. When we first heard about the Mozart effect, we became even more convinced that music should be part of our everyday lives. Books are another thing that is part of our daily lives. We always have a time when each of us reads on our own and a time when we read aloud to the others. Family time means spending time together, whatever it is that we are doing. When we do chores around the house, we always include our daughter. It may take more time to cook dinner or clean up when she helps, but we think that children learn important things like how to plan and implement plans when they are part of chores. So I guess our daughter's education is something that we think about and do something about every day of our lives (personal communication, Julie Johns, June 4, 2002).

ment or to the quality of a parent–child relationship, gay and lesbian families face unique issues of prejudice and the hurtful actions of others. In addition to these issues, gay and lesbian families face the same challenges of other family configurations discussed so far in this chapter—two-career families, blended families, and single-parent families—as well as other family types that will be discussed.

Families Raising Grandchildren

More than ever before, grandparents find themselves raising their grandchildren. The National Center for Health Statistics (Saluter, 1996) reported that 3.7 million children are currently being raised by grandparents. Most grandchildren move in with grandparents for one of the following reasons:

- ☑ Increasing numbers of single-parent families
- ☑ The high rate of divorce
- ☑ Teenage pregnancies

- ☑ AIDS
- ☑ Incarcerations of parents
- ☑ Substance abuse by parents
- ☑ Death or disability of parents
- ☑ Parental abuse and neglect (American Academy of Child and Adolescent Psychiatry, 2000)

Grandparents who are called on to raise a new family have special needs. They may feel anger, resentment, and maybe even guilt that their own children were not successful parents. The grandchildren may be coping with issues related to abuse or neglect, or the loss of parents. Beyond these emotional issues, many of these grandparents experience severe financial problems. More than 20% of grandparents raising their grandchildren live below the poverty line (Fields, 2001). Teachers who have students living with their grandparents may need to suggest that grandparents in this situation reach out for support and/or assistance. Family members, clergy, support groups, social agencies, and sources such as The Grandparents Information Center, sponsored by the American Association of Retired Persons, can be good resources (American Academy of Child and Adolescent Psychiatry, 2000).

VOICES *of Families*

I've raised my children. I'm retired. Instead of sleeping late and spending time with my friends, I'm up every morning getting two of my grandchildren ready for the school bus. Then it seems like they've just left when they're back home. They get home at 3:00, hungry. They are full of energy, but it's not really safe to let them play outside around here. I keep them in the apartment most of the time. A lot of times their noise gives me a real bad headache, but that doesn't matter if my head hurts. I still have to feed them dinner and make them take a bath and figure out what they are going to wear to school tomorrow. It's five or six hours before I can get them in bed. I'm just too old for this, but I'm all they've got.

I don't think about their school too much. They don't have homework. I'm always asking about homework, but they don't have any. They bother me to come up to eat lunch with them, but I make up some story when they ask me. I don't want to do that, all those kids and all that noise. I don't go to PTA meetings or carnivals or stuff like that. Now, I do go to those parent–teacher conferences they have, but that's about it (personal communication, Keisha Trainor, 21 May 2002).

Families with Adopted Children

Approximately 1.5 million children in the United States live with one or two parents who adopted them. Of this number, 35% live with one biological parent and one adoptive parent, 47% live with two adoptive parents, 16% live in single-parent families, and 2% live with one adoptive parent and one stepparent.

Children react to the concept that they are adopted in different ways. Some children accept their adoption as a matter of fact. Other children may deny the adoption. Many adopted children want to talk about their adoption, and teachers accept this discussion casually, just as they do other family-related topics. If a child seems to be experiencing emotional problems related to his or her adoption, teachers set an appointment with the parents and talk with them about how they can work together to support the child. There are many children's books about adoption. These can be helpful in starting conversations with a child about his or her feelings about being adopted. Over time, with open conversations about adoption, children's worries are less likely to develop (American Academy of Child and Adolescent Psychiatry, 1999a).

VOICES *of Families*

We were married for ten years and had been trying to get pregnant for five of those when we started looking into adoption. At first, I wanted a baby, a tiny baby, but we were told by more than one agency that we might have to wait up to four or five years. We weren't getting any younger. So, after talking about it for a couple of months, we agreed that we would adopt two children. In about six months, we got "the" phone call and two weeks after that, our family went from two people to four people, and things have never been the same. I don't even know if I can describe my role in my family. I have dozens of roles now. I used to think that I was busy, but now I am a mom, a teacher, a tutor, a psychologist, a play therapist, a nurse, a dietitian, a cook, a waitress, a maid, and that's all before they finish breakfast.

So, when it comes to their educations, I am committed to helping them become the best they can be. I feel fortunate that my kids have teachers who understand. They let me come into the classroom just about whenever I want to. I work with my children, but I always include other children too. I feel like I am helping children learn more than they might otherwise, but I'm really doing it so that I know what my kids are studying and how they are doing in class. I am going to take what they are learning at school and extend it as much as I can. So if my youngest is studying zoo animals, that Saturday I plan a trip for us to the zoo. I check out books about zoo animals and we read those after school every day. I have them draw pictures and write stories and we count things every day (personal communication, Pam Elliott, 29 May 2002).

Families with Foster Children

The number of children who live in foster families continues to increase. Almost 600,000 children currently live with foster parents, which represents an increase of 48% over the past decade (Children's Defense Fund, 2001). Children in foster care have been removed from their homes by a child welfare agency, frequently because of abuse and neglect. Other reasons for placement in a foster home include abandonment by the biological parents; parental illness, either physical or emotional; alcohol or substance abuse; and death.

African American children represent almost 66% of children in foster care and they tend to remain in foster care for longer periods of time. Most children, two out of three, are reunited with their birth parents within twenty-four months, although children who are available for adoption can spend much longer in foster care.

Being removed from their home and parents and placed in a foster home is particularly stressful for children. Some of the issues children in foster care address are

- ☑ Blaming themselves and feeling guilty about removal from their birth parents
- ☑ Wishing to return to birth parents even if they were abused by them
- ☑ Feeling unwanted if awaiting adoption for a long time
- ☑ Feeling helpless about multiple changes in foster parents over time

VOICES of Families

The children who live with me really need me. Each one of them has their own story, but abuse and neglect are part of all of their stories. They don't trust adults, and for good reason. So, I see my job as earning their trust. I need to give them a safe place to live where they know that I'll always be there when they need me, whether it's getting them clothes or fixing foods they like to eat or just when they need to talk about something. I set up a schedule so they know when we eat, when we play, when we do chores, when we take baths, and when we go to sleep. They need that sense of security and it's my job to see that they get it.

As to my role in the children's educations, that is different. I try to go up to the schools and have lunch with them once or twice a year. That makes the kids feel special, like they really belong to us. I may go to a PTA meeting here and there, but other than that—and supervising homework—that is about all I do. Right now we have six foster children and taking care of their needs here at home is pretty time-consuming. That doesn't leave much time for a lot of volunteer work in their schools (personal communication, Breanna Martinez, 14 May 2002).

☑ Having mixed emotions about attaching to foster parents
☑ Feeling insecure and uncertain about their future
☑ Reluctantly acknowledging positive feelings for foster parents (American Academy of Child and Adolescent Psychiatry, 2002)

Teachers who have students living in foster homes may be called on to refer the foster parents to community resources. It helps to be knowledgeable about what resources are locally available.

Families with Children with Special Needs

Families who have children with special needs have their own needs, and these are just as varied as the special needs that children have. Some are focused on ensuring that the child receives the medical attention required for the child's condition. Some

VOICES *of Families*

For a long time, we were about the same as most families. My wife did the grocery shopping and cooking. I paid the bills and took out the garbage. We took on those roles when we first got married, doing pretty much what we had seen our parents do. But those gender-related roles went out the window when our first child was born. He has Down's syndrome. So now we have to do all the things that every family has to do, and we are totally focused on supporting our child so he can become the best, most accomplished person he can be. Today, we know that children with Down's syndrome can grow up to be relatively independent. They go to high school and sometimes even college. We want him to have all these advantages, so we work with him every day, every day. Children with Down's syndrome have certain tendencies. They have low muscle tone, which often leads to obesity. They have heart defects more than most

children. They are more likely to develop asthma, diabetes, hypertension, hypothyroidism, and a lot more, so we plan things and support his physical development and cognitive development more than we would a child who was not challenged by Down's syndrome.

As far as his education goes, I think we don't depend on teachers the way a lot of parents do. We really see ourselves as partners with his teacher, and we let teachers know that up front. We have a conference with his teacher every week or two just to track how he is doing in his class—he is in kindergarten—and to see if we are all seeing the same progress, and to see if there are new things we should be doing with him at home to support his progress at school. We are determined to keep him in a regular classroom, and we are willing to spend as much time as it takes to do that (personal communication, Demarrion Jackson 29 May 2002).

cannot provide all the care that their child requires, and they are focused on coordinating care among agencies, organizations, and volunteers.

Homeless Families

More than 700,000 people are homeless on any given night, and up to 2 million people experience homelessness during one year (National Law Center on Homelessness and Poverty, 1999). Thousands of these people are young children. The McKinney Homeless Assistance Act of 1987 guarantees that homeless children will have access to education; however, this does not ensure that these children actually attend child care or elementary schools.

The teachers of those homeless children who do attend schools face unique challenges. The lack of a place to live is usually just the beginning of a family's problems. Homelessness is often accompanied by abuse, depression, and poverty. Teachers can provide support for homeless families when they are familiar with various social and health services in the community. These families almost always qualify for many support services: physical and mental health services, child care for young children, after-school care for elementary students, and possibly transportation arrangements. But, even though they qualify, they often do not know how to access community services. Teachers or other school support staff can help families contact agencies and complete the necessary paperwork (Swartz, 1995).

All of the adults whose voices are represented in this chapter are rearing children who are cared for at a child care center or attend public school. Even though the family configurations are different, they discuss common issues: taking care of children's basic needs, spending time with their children, and keeping children busy at home. Their statements about family involvement range from significant involvement to parents and other caregivers who are not involved at all in their children's school or education.

It is important for educators to become familiar with the types of families their students have. If teachers understand the demands faced by different families, they can work with them more effectively. Having realistic expectations for different family configurations allows teachers and schools to develop programs that facilitate partnerships between home and school, promote better communication, and develop more meaningful involvement.

VOICES *of Families*

I'm not sure what my role is in my family anymore. Six months ago, I would have said things like provider, cook, disciplinarian, but now, I don't know. I was laid off from my job and had no savings, so here I am in a homeless shelter with my two little girls. I am trying to get back to being responsible for those things a mother should do. I want to help my kids learn. I know I should be working with them when they get out of school. But every night, I am so tired that I end up just sitting in the community room and watching TV (personal communication, Shenekwa Brown, 7 May 2002).

Summary

Today's families are very different in their configurations and in how they live their lives. Yet, as different as they are, they share similarities, namely, meeting the needs of their children.

 ## Reflections

1. Consider what these family members said about their roles at home and their role in their child's education. Discuss the similarities and the differences among these individuals.
2. This chapter only discusses different structures of families. Create a list of other characteristics of families and how those characteristics might affect parents' thoughts or feelings about being involved in their children's educations.

 ## Field Experiences

1. Survey several families using the same open-ended questions of "Tell me a little about your role in your family" and "How do you view your role in your child's education?" Share the results with peers. Try to determine any similarities within and among different family configurations.

 ## Other Activities

1. Invite a school counselor to talk about different types of families and strategies that the counselor has found to be effective in involving families at school.
2. Invite representative members of families from the different family structures discussed in this chapter to lead a panel discussion of the needs of different family types and how teachers can best help these families become involved in their children's education/school experience.

 ## Further Readings

Nord, C. W. (1998). *Father involvement in schools.* ERIC Digest. ERIC Reproduction Document Number 419632.

   This article examines the extent of family involvement of fathers in all configurations of families and suggests ways that educators can encourage more involvement from fathers.

Roe, K. M., & Minkler, M. (1998/99). Grandparents raising grandchildren: Challenges and responses. *Generations, 22,* 25–33.

   This article gives a profile of the typical caregiving grandparents, outlines challenges faced by these grandparents, and suggests support services for them.

Swartz, W. (1995). *School programs and practices for homeless students.* (Report No. EDO-UD-95-2). Washington, DC: Office of Educational Research and Improvement, U.S. Department of Education. (ERIC Document Reproduction Service Digest No. 105)

   This digest identifies several characteristics of homeless students and suggests what schools and teachers can do to support these children.

Schwartz, W. (1999). *Family diversity in urban schools.* ERIC Digest. ERIC Reproduction Document Number 434188

   This digest identifies several common types of nontraditional families and presents a few of their characteristics relevant to their children's education.

Schwartz, W. (1999). School support for foster families. ERIC Digest. ERIC Reproduction Document Number 434189

   Factors that influence the ability of foster children to be successful in school are detailed. Schwartz offers strategies that teachers and schools can use to improve foster children's educational success and emotional well-being.

Swick, K. J., & Graves, S. B. (1993). *Empowering at-risk families during the early childhood years.* Washington, DC: National Education Association.

Swick and Graves define the characteristics of families at-risk and discuss in detail how educators can relate to the needs of at-risk families and support them.

Websites to Explore

- Administration for Children and Families
370 L'Enfant Promenade SW
Washington, DC 20447
http://www.acf.dhhs.gov/
- Families and Work Institute
267 Fifth Ave., Floor 2
New York, NY 10016
Phone: (212) 465-2044
Fax: (212) 465-8637
http://www.familiesandwork.org/

- Federation for Children with Special Needs
1135 Tremont Street, Suite 420
Boston, Massachusetts 02120
617-236-7210
Fax 617-572-2094
http://www.fcsn.org/
- Human Rights Campaign Foundation: Family Network
919 18th St., N.W., Suite 800
Washington, DC 20006
202-628-4160
Fax: 202-347-5323
http://www.hrc.org/familynet/
- Parents Without Partners
1650 South Dixie Highway, Suite 510
Boca Raton, FL 33432
561-391-8833
Fax: 561-395-8557
http://parentswithoutpartners.org

3

What Teachers Say about Family Involvement

Learning Objectives

The reader will learn and be able to discuss:

- The continuum of beliefs about family involvement held by early childhood educators
- The relationship between beliefs about family involvement and actual practices
- Factors that affect teachers' beliefs about family involvement

> Teacher attributes that appear to positively influence teachers' relationships with children and parents include: warmth, openness, sensitivity, flexibility, reliability, and accessibility.
>
> —James Comer and M. Haynes, 1991

As much diversity exists among teachers' opinions regarding family involvement as exists among families. When asked about their beliefs on family involvement, most teachers respond with comments that mirror the opinions of experts. Teachers talk about how children benefit when the school and the home work together. Many even quote research that says children are more successful in school when their families are involved in their education—that attendance goes up, children are more interested in school work, and their grades are better when families are involved.

When asked whether or not teachers should be expected to work with families, their answers are varied, but most say they think teachers should work with families (Diffily, 2000).

Beliefs about Working with Families

When asked the question "What are ways you believe early childhood educators should work with families of the children they teach?" 91% of early childhood educators responded with at least one way they believed teachers should work with families. Twenty-seven percent of early childhood educators responded with complex answers indicating that they believed teachers should use many forms of family involvement (Diffily, 2000). Some of their answers follow:

☑ We must realize we are in partnership with the families, so communication between us is vitally important for the development of the child. Newsletters, conferences, family nights are all ways we are currently involving our families in their child's education. We encourage (but do not require) volunteers in the classrooms.

☑ Communication, understanding, listening, caring, lending advice, education.

☑ By assuming a *collaborative* partnership, relationship, listening to parent concerns and answering those concerns in a nonsuperior attitude, jargon free. Determine common goals.

☑ Invite them into your classroom with an open door policy, do home visits, provide parenting information, developmental and educational information on a

Diffily, 2000, refers to a survey about beliefs and practices of early childhood educators about working with families completed by 382 educators at the October 2000 annual conference of the Texas Association for the Education of Young Children and in-depth follow-up interviews with fifty-three volunteer respondents.

regular basis in nonthreatening mode, plan social occasions events, ask them to share family traditions.

☑ Educators make one-on-one personal, informal contact with parents to encourage communication, send home weekly letters, hold conferences—at least 30 minutes—have helping hands meetings where parents and teachers cut and laminate items to make games while they talk to each other.

☑ Become a trusted friend. Be a listener. Involve the family in activities at the school.

☑ Absolutely imperative to work with families in different ways. We work sometimes as much with teaching parents as we do with their young children. We send letters home, encourage parents to come to classes with their children to share in activities, talk with parents in the mornings and afternoons, call them at home, share with them in all kinds of ways, whatever works best for our families.

Twelve percent of teachers answered the same question "What are ways you believe early childhood educators should work with families of the children they teach?" in shorter statements that indicated their belief that the teacher's work with families was limited to one-way communication; their responsibility was to inform families. These responses included

☑ Educate them!
☑ Sit down and explain reasons their children act certain ways.
☑ Inform parents of what you are working on with their children both verbally and in written form.
☑ Give them basic curriculum on your activities.
☑ Tell them things to do at home.
☑ Teach parents what to do with their young children.
☑ Advise on parenting techniques.

A few teachers, less than 2%, saw family involvement only in terms of what parents could do for teachers or the school. Their answers included

☑ Buying supplies that are needed.
☑ Encourage them to volunteer in the classroom. Send home things that they can cut out.
☑ Assist with activities and materials for the classroom.
☑ The parents can come in and volunteer their time in the classroom working with other children as well as their own.
☑ By having them bring their things they have about their different heritages.

On the furthest end of the continuum of beliefs, some early childhood educators view their professional obligations as being only with the children. Nine percent of the early childhood educators responded that they did not believe they should have to work with families. Most of these teachers indicated that they did not have enough time to do everything they did for children and still have time to work with families. Some of their responses included

☑ I don't feel comfortable working with adults. That is why I teach young children.

☑ I don't think I should have to try and make my parents better parents. I teach children, not parenting skills.

☑ I think there should be a parent educator. There is not enough time in the day to teach little children and to work with their parents.

Working with Families

Some teachers define family involvement in very narrow ways and a few do not see their responsibility to encourage family involvement at all, but the vast majority of early childhood educators believe they should encourage family involvement to some degree. However, this strong support for family involvement is not borne out in individual practices. When asked specific questions about their own practices, most teachers actually do less with families than their beliefs indicate.

When asked how much time they spend working with families and what kinds of methods they use to communicate with and involve families, teachers' answers are less supportive of family involvement than their beliefs. When asked about the amount of time they spend working with families, teacher's answers are varied. Some teachers devote some time every day to communicating and working with families, but most teachers say they spend little or no time working with families on a weekly basis (Diffily, 2000). Many factors affect what teachers actually do with families.

Factors Affecting Work with Families

Many early childhood educators feel that their work with children comes easily to them, but that working with families is much harder (Diffily, 2000). In a 1997 study about parent involvement, Amy Baker found that many teachers see working with parents as one of the hardest parts of their job. When interviewed, Baker said, "You can't believe how strongly and how negatively teachers feel toward parents. They don't really enjoy interacting with parents, and partly at least, it's because they're not trained . . ." (Jones, 2001).

Types of Educational Programs

The type of early childhood program that teachers work in has a direct affect on the time they dedicate to working with families. When the program places a strong emphasis on family involvement, teachers spend more time working with the families of children in the program. Teachers live up to the expectations that are set for them by administrators and nurtured by other teachers within the program. They tend to adopt the practices of other teachers within the program. When other

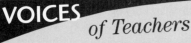

VOICES of Teachers

I work with parents every day. But then not every teacher can do it the way that I do. I work part-time in the afternoons when parents come to pick up their children. That's when I get to talk to parents: about their child, about their family, about good things they need to be doing with their kids, about lots of things.

Pickup time is very different from drop off time. In the mornings, most parents are in a big hurry, trying to get to work on time. I could not work with families like I do if I worked mornings. And afternoon pickup time in child care centers is different than in public school. We don't have one dismissal time like public schools. Parents drop in at different times, so there is more time for that relaxed talk about children. Another thing I have going for me is my age. I'm kind of a grandmother figure for lots of the mothers here. They'll talk to me—and listen to what I have to say—because I am that grandmotherly type of person. I think that is particularly true for the young mothers who are living a long way from their own mothers. I can say things like, "You ought to be shutting off that TV and reading with your child, every night, every night!" If some of the younger teachers said that very same thing, parents might think the teacher was being bossy and get upset.

teachers write weekly letters to families and have regular meetings with family members, then teachers new to that program adopt those practices.

Early childhood education has many types of programs: preschools, child care centers (both nonprofit and for profit), Head Start programs, private schools, public schools, charter schools, and parent cooperative schools. There is as much diversity within each type of program as there is among the different types. However, it is generally true that family involvement is more common in parent cooperative schools and Head Start programs than in the other types of early childhood programs.

In parent cooperative schools, families are required to be involved in the life of the school and in their children's classes. James Hymes, former president of the National Association for the Education of Young Children, described family involvement in cooperative programs in the following way:

> Co-op mothers and fathers take their school responsibilities seriously. They read books and articles and pamphlets about early childhood development and education. They meet often for parent discussions. It has been said—but the people weren't complaining, just describing: "Co-ops are the meeting-est places!" Mothers and fathers confer frequently with the teacher. Most important

of all, parents work directly in the classroom with the children, as aides or teacher-assistants or parent-helpers—whatever word you want to use. On a regular basis, co-op parents see their child's behavior in the group, they see other children's behavior, they see a school program at work (http://www.ccppns.org/notes.html).

Parent cooperative schools exist in many states in many different types of schools. However, most co-ops are in preschools.

Head Start programs are federally funded programs designed to meet the education and health needs of low-income three- to five-year-old children and their families. Head Start began in 1965 in the Office of Economic Opportunity and is now administered by the Administration for Children and Families. Parental involvement is an essential part of all Head Start programs. Parental involvement includes classes and workshops about child development issues, school-based and home-based programs that help adults understand appropriate educational activities for young children, and having a voice about the operations of the program.

Many charter schools have strong family involvement components, but this occurs on a school-by-school basis. By definition, a charter school is a public school freed from most state statutes and regulations. It is organized by a group of teachers, parents, and/or community members with specific goals and operating procedures that are spelled out in the charter. Legislation governing charter schools is created at the state level. Although no state requires a specific family involvement component to approve the application for a charter school, encouraging parent/community involvement in public schools is usually considered an intention in charter school legislation.

Some public schools, outside the charter school movement, are now requesting that families donate a certain number of hours to the school each year. Early in the school year, each family receives a list of the different ways that they can volunteer at the school. The list covers a wide range of opportunities for parents, such as answering the telephone in the school office, helping children in the library, monitoring children in the cafeteria, serving on various committees, planning fund-raising events, tutoring children, and organizing clubs for children.

Just as family involvement is important in some public schools, it is also fostered in some preschools and child care centers. However, strong family involvement is typically the exception rather than the rule.

Insufficient Training

Training is also a factor in how much family involvement teachers encourage. Early childhood educators indicated that they are not always confident about how they should go about working with families (Diffily, 2000). When questioned, most say that there was little or no attention given to working with families in their college

VOICES of Teachers

In my college classes, I had learned that families were critically important to their children's success at school. We learned about different ways to work with families. We had all kinds of assignments in our classes that related to working with families. We wrote letters about different educational issues. We created newsletters and set up websites. We planned family meetings and role played conferences. After several classes, I came to understand that working with families was just part of my responsibilities as a teacher.

Then I got my first job. The reality of what happened at that school was so different from what I learned in college classes. Parents were not involved in that school at all. They didn't come to PTA meetings. They didn't come to conferences. They rarely even came into the building. It was so strange to me.

After two or three weeks, it dawned on me. Parents weren't involved in that school because they were not invited to do that. Teachers did not approach parents for any kind of conversation before or after school. They did not send home anything except what the office told them to. It was like the teachers at this school almost put up walls between themselves and the families of students. No wonder parents stayed away from classrooms.

courses. A University of Minnesota survey seems to support this opinion. More than 1,100 principals and superintendents were asked how well new teachers were prepared for their professional responsibilities. For items such as teaching in the content areas, survey respondents indicated 73% of new teachers were well prepared or very well prepared. In contrast, the survey showed that only 25% of new teachers were well prepared or very well prepared to work with parents (Jones, 2001).

Insufficient Time

Time is a factor in what early childhood educators actually do in working with the families of their students. Teachers often express a desire to have more family involvement (McWilliam and Maxwell, 1999). Yet, when asked why they believe families are not more involved in their classes or with their child's education, the answer typically has something to do with time. Teachers discuss the fact that they do not have enough time to keep up with teaching children while spending enough time with families to keep them interested and involved. They also talk about the busy lives that families lead today. They say involvement in school takes a lower priority than other things in the family's life.

Insufficient Resources

Many early childhood educators say that in addition to not having enough time to work with families, they do not receive sufficient support (Diffily, 2000). Some teachers complain of very simple things such as having a copy machine available when they need it. Others complain of larger issues such as administrators not wanting teachers and families in the building at night, which limits the kinds of meetings and activities teachers are able to schedule.

Some teachers complain that they do not have the support of administrators. Many teachers think that administrators could show their support for family involvement if they hired subs so that teachers could hold family–teacher conferences or family meetings during the day during their regular working hours. Others think that administrators should find the money to support family meetings by things such as buying food for those who attend the meetings. Several believe that more parents would come to the school if all the classes had family meetings, but that administrators are reluctant to tell all the teachers to hold these kinds of meetings.

Several teachers believe that they need resources to support their work with families. In a recent survey, early childhood educators indicated that within the last six months, they had asked for the following resources and had yet to receive them:

- ☑ Help with time management issues
- ☑ A teacher assistant
- ☑ Funding for workshops that relate to family involvement
- ☑ Time to spend with other teachers or schools that have strong family involvement
- ☑ Videotapes that show effective parenting strategies
- ☑ Information about various cultural influences on families
- ☑ Collections of articles about specific issues
- ☑ Resource pamphlets about different parenting issues to share with families
- ☑ Resource books about how to coordinate meetings with families,
- ☑ Books with quick and easy ideas for families and children to do at home
- ☑ Books and other materials to share with families (i.e. a lending library)

VOICES *of Teachers*

I know the families of my students pretty well. I don't think that they purposefully sit down and say to themselves, "We are going to put education on our list of priorities below soccer, tee–ball, friends, video games, and television." Although I think if they were honest with themselves, that is exactly where they place education in their lives. They spend all kinds of time driving to sports practices and games and helping their children practice at home. Playing on one sports team can take up to three afternoons or evenings a week, plus one weekend day. They would think I was crazy if I asked that they spend that much time every week in our classroom or working with their child at home.

☑ Mental health professionals to answer questions about individual families
☑ Lists of local agencies that provide services needed by families in the program

Each of these teachers believed that they could do more with families if they had these additional resources.

Insufficient Parental Interest

When discussing family involvement, approximately half of early childhood educators indicate that they would be willing to do more work with families if families showed more interest (Diffily, 2000). Conversations in teachers' lounges or comments made during seminars about family involvement might lead you to believe that most teachers are rather negative about family involvement. That is, they seem negative about families not being as involved as they think they should. The following comments are not unusual:

☑ The students and I spent two whole days getting ready for Open House night. We all cleaned the room and decorated it. The children put together their special papers in a folder to share with their parents. How many show up? One aunt, and she only came in the room for 10 minutes. For the rest of the 2 hours, I was alone in the classroom. Why bother?

☑ Why do we even work on these PTA plays? Hardly any of the parents show up. It just sets the children up for disappointment. At school, they work on these plays. They practice and practice. Then, the night of the play, they can't get their parents to bring them to the school.

☑ I've stopped sending home family homework. They never send it back.

☑ I go to the trouble of writing a letter to families every week. That takes me about an hour every Thursday night of my life. You can imagine how I feel on Monday mornings when I go through the children's folders and see the letters still there in the folders. No one even bothered to take it out of the folder, much less read it.

☑ I offer to meet families at school, in their homes, or somewhere neutral, like the public library or a restaurant. Still, less than half of the families of my students even respond to my notes or my phone calls. It is frustrating. I don't know what more I can do. If the parents are not interested, I can't make them come to a conference, can I?

VOICES *of Teachers*

I taught ten years in an inner city school where no one worked very hard to reach out to families. It was sort of assumed that they would not respond, so no one on the faculty did much with parents—except complain about them. Then I came to the school where I work now. It is also an urban school, with pretty much the same population as the first school where I taught, but it is very different here.

Here it is assumed that teachers will go out of their way to make families feel comfortable in our school and create opportunities for families to come to the school. In many ways, it was a culture shock for me.

The teacher's experience described in the box opposite is not isolated. Sometimes families really do not care, but more often, teachers incorrectly perceive that parents are not interested in their children's education. Too often, families who have different lifestyles or who hold different values from teachers are seen as uncaring or ineffective parents (Swick, 1996), and these beliefs are often a major barrier in positive relationships between teachers and families (Galinsky, 1990; Powell, 1989).

Some teachers cite research that seems to support their belief that today's parents are not providing the kinds of experiences at home that support a child's academic success. Data from the National Assessment of Educational Progress (NAEP) indicates that three factors account for almost 90% of the difference in the average state-by-state performance of older children's mathematics scores. The three factors are student absenteeism, the variety of reading materials in the home, and excessive television watching. Families have control over these factors, not teachers.

Summary

There is a wide range of teacher beliefs about what they should be doing related to working with families, as well as a wide range of actual practices. Most teachers believe they would be doing more with families if they had the kind of support they need and if families showed more interest.

Reflections

1. Think back to the teachers of your early childhood years. Talk to your family about these teachers and ways that they encouraged or discouraged the involvement of family members. From their actions, what beliefs about family involvement would you imagine they held?
2. If you believed—as some teachers in this chapter indicated—that the parents of your students "didn't care," consider how that would affect your willingness to continue reaching out to parents.
3. If other teachers in your program did not see working with families as part of their responsibili-

ties, how might this affect your personal practices? Go back and read the box on page 36. Think about what you would do if you were this teacher.

Field Experiences

1. Talk with two or three teachers about their feelings about family involvement and their reasons for actively encouraging or not encouraging families to be involved in their classes.
2. Ask four teachers what kind of resources they would need to increase their work with families. Compile answers from all teachers and determine teachers' greatest need.

Other Activities

1. Spend some time estimating how long it would take you every week to do the following activities related to working with families: writing one letter to all the families, writing individual notes to three families, making three telephone calls, and having one parent/teacher conference. In small groups, talk about how this amount of time might affect your decision of how much to work with families.

Further Reading

Gorter-Reu, M. S., & Anderson, J. M. (1998). Home kits, home visits, and more! *Young Children, 53,* 71–74.

This article recommends several concrete ways that teachers can involve families in their children's educations.

Kaufman, H. O. (2001). Skills for working with all families. *Young Children, 56,* 81–83.

Kaufman looks at family involvement from the perspective of what skills teachers need to make families feel wanted and comfortable.

Survival Guide for New Teachers: Working with Parents http://www.ed.gov/pubs/survivalguide/parent.html.

Written from the perspective of teachers reaching out to families, this brief paper offers solid suggestions for developing relationships with families.

Website to Explore

■ Partnership for Learning http://www.partnershipforlearning.org/ (Go to www.partnershipforlearning.org/article.asp? ArticleID=287 for an article about what teachers wish families knew about working as partners)

4

Reluctant Families, Reluctant Teachers

Learning Objectives

The reader will learn and be able to discuss:

- Several barriers that families face in becoming involved in their children's educations
- Ways to overcome these barriers
- Several barriers that teachers face in helping families becoming involved in their children's educations
- Ways to overcome these barriers

> Parent–teacher relationships . . . are complex things, uniting two sets of internal experiences, needs, and responses with two sets of external circumstances.
>
> —Carol Gestwicki, 2000

As seen in the first three chapters, most experts, families, and teachers discuss family involvement in very positive ways. Each group acknowledges that all parties, especially the children, benefit when the home and the school work together. However, these positive attitudes are most often expressed when the topic is being discussed in the global sense. When the subject of family involvement is brought down to the classroom level, the actions of individual family members and teachers do not always mirror the favorable attitudes expressed by each of those groups. What sounds good in theory—families and teachers working together—is not always easy to accomplish in practice.

Not every family is ready and willing to be active in their child's education, at home or at school, and not every teacher is willing to open the classroom to families or reach out to family members to involve them in the life of the class. Knowing that concerns exist on both parts helps people understand what to expect when beginning family involvement programs. Educators may recognize some of the following concerns in family members and in themselves.

Families Reluctant to Become Involved

The vast majority of families want what is best for their children. If they understood how much their children would benefit by their involvement in the school, they might be more inclined to become involved. However, there are many reasons that families do not automatically volunteer to participate in school activities. Many adults are simply uncomfortable in school settings. Others are fearful of being judged by their child's teacher. Still others would like to be involved in their child's education, but they are unable to work out the logistics of getting to the school. Often, the time the teacher sets for family involvement activities is inconvenient—school activities conflict with work responsibilities. Many families do not have a car and cannot work out public transportation from their homes to the school. Other families face the issue of child care. Making arrangements for younger siblings can be difficult and taking toddlers or preschoolers to school may be awkward. Sometimes it seems impossible to work out all the logistics so at least one parent can be involved in the child's class. Most of the barriers to family involvement can be overcome. But first, the reasons families are reluctant to be involved at school need to be identified.

Feeling Uncomfortable at School

For many adults simply walking into a school building brings back memories of their own elementary school classes, and school was not a positive experience for everyone. Some adults actually feel like they did as second-graders who had not finished their homework, or as fourth-graders who got in trouble for talking at the wrong times. Other adults see a principal's office and suddenly feel panicked that someone is going to call their mothers. These negative emotions are illogical, but nonetheless real. If parents hated school when they were children or have unpleasant memories of their early schooling, it is unlikely that they feel comfortable about spending much time in a classroom as an adult.

OVERCOMING THIS BARRIER   Teachers are responsible for reaching out to families and helping break down barriers that prevent families from becoming involved in the classroom. For adults who feel uncomfortable in schools, the most obvious way to help is to create a warm and inviting classroom environment. Chances are the bad memories are associated with a regimented classroom where all the desks were in rows and all the students were expected to work in silence. Imagine one of these adults walking into a classroom where plants are scattered through the room, walls are filled with children's work, tables are strategically arranged for small group work, and baskets of books are placed in every learning center. This kind of classroom does not look like or feel like the classrooms in their elementary school memories. Beyond an inviting classroom environment, teachers also need to be warm and inviting. When teachers communicate an open-door policy and families feel that the teacher truly wants them in the classroom, many adults will change how they feel about being in schools. Instead of feeling uncomfortable, over time, families will feel welcome in classrooms and actually enjoy the time they spend there.

Fear of Being Judged

Other families avoid their child's classroom because they worry about being judged. They often see the teacher as an educated person, above them in social status. They worry about how the classroom teacher may perceive them. They worry about not having nice clothes to wear to school. They worry about saying the wrong thing, or in the case of second-language parents, worry that they will not communicate so that they are understood. Some families do not see themselves as competent and fear being asked to participate in activities that they feel unprepared for (Rockwell, Andre, and Hawley, 1995). This is especially true of poor families, families from diverse cultural and language backgrounds, and parents who have minimal educational backgrounds and skills. It is often difficult to get these family members into the classroom so the teacher can help them overcome these negative feelings.

OVERCOMING THIS BARRIER Again, teachers have the primary responsibility for overcoming this barrier to family involvement. Teachers reach out to families in many ways, but there are two important ways to eliminate a family's feeling that they might be judged. The first is a regular written communication with families in which the tone is friendly, open, and caring. Through reading letters and notes from the teacher, these families begin to see the teacher as someone who cares enough about them to keep them informed about the class. Through the tone of the letters, families may begin to think that this teacher is one they could approach without feeling judged. The second way to help eliminate these negative feelings is to get the families into the classroom. Even if every letter sent home includes an invitation to drop in to the class at any time, reluctant families may not take advantage of that open-door policy. However, if an invitation goes home to a specific event—the children reciting poetry, performing a simple play, or sharing their latest science experiment—some of these families may risk coming to school just to see their child's work.

The most effective invitation to the classroom is the teacher calling (or speaking with) a family and asking them to do something specific. A mother who has a low self-image and fears being judged by the teacher might risk coming to school if the teacher specifically asks her to help the children make pancakes after reading *Pancakes, Pancakes* by Eric Carle (1998), or help peel apples to make applesauce. The idea that the teacher asked them to do something they feel able to do may be just the action to help families come into the classroom for the first time. Then, once in the classroom, it is up to the teacher to be open, kind, and grateful, reinforcing the idea that she truly wants all families involved in the life of the classroom.

Fear of Hearing Bad News

In addition to less-than-happy memories of their own elementary school days, less-than-happy experiences with their older children often make families reluctant to communicate with the teacher. Many families feel that they hear from the school only when something is wrong. Some teachers call home only to report some infraction on the part of the child or write a note to explain some wrong-doing. When this is true, parents do not look forward to hearing from the teacher, and then families carry this negative feeling about communication to subsequent teachers.

OVERCOMING THIS BARRIER Perhaps this is the easiest barrier to remove. From the beginning of school, teachers who make telephone calls to each family just to say that they are pleased their child is in the class establish a personal relationship

VOICES of Families

With Jake, my first child, I heard from his teacher—a lot. It felt like she called me every single time that Jake touched another child or talked when he wasn't supposed to. At first, I was embarrassed. I would talk to Jake and he would promise to be better. But she just kept calling. She never had anything good to say about him. It was frustrating. I never wanted to step foot in that class.

So, when Jennifer's teacher called that first week of school, I thought, "Here we go again."

But Mrs. Gonzales called to tell me how much she was enjoying Jennifer, and she told me a couple of stories about how Jennifer had helped other children in the class. Just that one phone call made me feel like she cared about my child and about me. When Mrs. Gonzales called a couple of weeks later to ask if I could help out with a cooking activity in class, I didn't hesitate to say, "Yes." What a difference in how I felt about going into my children's classrooms, and it was all because of how the teacher made me feel.

with that family. These telephone calls need not be long. The primary purpose is to let families know how much the teacher cares about the students and to make a positive impression on the family. When trying to break down this barrier with families who avoid communication, teachers send home notes about individual children. They ensure that each family receives two or three positive notes before a note describing a problem goes home. These notes do not need to be long. A couple of sentences, written during a lunch break, is sufficient to impress families about how the teacher is trying to communicate good things about their child.

Issues of Time, Transportation, Child Care, and Other Logistical Problems

The logistics of getting from their homes to the school prevents some parents from getting involved in their child's class. There are many issues that have to be worked out to free up some time when adults can go to the school and spend time in their child's classroom. One issue is time, when the teacher schedules the opportunities for family involvement. If the only time the teacher asks for help is first thing in the morning, and a parent's job requires that he or she be on the job at 8 A.M., then that parent is left out.

Parents have to juggle all their responsibilities. For some, the issue is not just when the volunteer opportunities are scheduled, but time itself. Families live very busy lives, trying to meet work responsibilities and the needs of all family members. They may want to be involved in their child's life at school, but choose to spend their free time during the day running errands for the family so they can spend their free time during the evening with their children.

Even when families have the time to become involved in their child's classroom, some parents have trouble with transportation from their home to the school. They may not have a car. Public transportation may not serve their area of town. And, the family may be new to the community and not know anyone they feel comfortable enough with to ask for a ride to the school. The issue of transportation is difficult; however, the classroom teacher can make some suggestions for parents to consider.

When families have more than one child, there is always the issue of child care. Many parents have trouble figuring out what to do with younger siblings. They can't afford drop-in child care costs. They don't have close friends that they would trust to care for their children while they go to the school. Taking young siblings into the child's classroom may not be an option. If child care is the issue preventing families from getting involved, this problem could affect every day of the school year. Parents would benefit from some ideas from the teacher.

Other logistics families face are job responsibilities and juggling the schedules of several children. The more a teacher gets to know individual families, the more aware she will be of some of the barriers a particular family faces. Then she can offer families some specific options that they might not have considered.

OVERCOMING THIS BARRIER Logistical barriers are a bit more difficult for the teacher to break down; however, there are a few things a teacher can do and some others that she can suggest to families. At the very least, the teacher can schedule opportunities for family involvement at different times of the day. This way more families have the chance to arrange their schedules so they can volunteer at school. Referring back to the parent who has to be on the job at 8 A.M., if the teacher also had a different opportunity around the noon hour, this parent might take a few more minutes for

VOICES *of Families*

I want to be a part of my child's education. I want to spend time in her class so that I can know the kids she talks about and learn the songs she sings. School is so important to her, and I want her to know that it is important to me too. But I am constantly facing some problem or another which makes it really hard for me to get to the school. We only have the one car. I know I could get up early and take my husband to work, but that means getting all three girls out of bed before 6 A.M. It's a forty-five-minute drive to his work—one way—so that means an hour and a half in the morning and then an hour and a half in the evening to pick him back up. Even if I arrange that, I have to find a place to leave the other two girls. I think I could take the baby into a kindergarten class without much problem, but the two-year-old does nothing but run around the room and I run around after her. I want to go to the school, but it is just so hard.

lunch and drive to school to spend some time. Teachers are typically sensitive to this logistical problem and work with parents according to their schedules.

The teacher cannot solve transportation or child care problems on her own. But, she can introduce families to each other. Perhaps they can work out agreements among themselves about offering rides to school or taking turns caring for younger siblings.

Personal Issues

Many times the reasons families do not get involved in their children's class have nothing to do with negative feelings about school or not being able to work out the logistics of getting to the school. Most families today live hectic lives, and few of us know all of the issues that another family copes with. Some families care for an elderly relative, which can be a time-consuming responsibility. Some families experience financial difficulties and have to take on second, or even third, jobs. Many families face problems that they are not willing to share with their child's teacher.

OVERCOMING THIS BARRIER   Teachers cannot help break down a barrier to family involvement that they do not even know about, but they do not intrude into families' privacy by asking inappropriate questions. By being supportive, and sometimes sympathetic, teachers establish a relationship with the families. Teachers continue to keep families informed about the class, invite them into the class, and trust that the family will get involved when they can.

Teachers Reluctant to Involve Families

Families are not the only ones who are reluctant to become involved at school. Just as many teachers are reluctant to have parents involved in the class. Some teachers believe their job is to teach children—only. They do not see working with families as part of their responsibility. Some teachers simply feel uncomfortable when someone watches them teach, and other teachers react negatively to adults visiting in their classrooms because they fear being criticized. Other teachers just do not know how to work with parent volunteers. Rather than feel uncomfortable, these teachers simply avoid parents.

Belief That Working with Families Is Not Their Job

Teachers who never explored the benefits of involving families generally do not understand just how important this work can be. Teachers who have never studied the logistics of involving families may not have a clue where to begin. Many teachers have never observed an active parent involvement program. Without understanding the benefits to everyone involved, and without knowing how to go about involving families, many teachers simply do not see working with families as part of their job. They think it would be very time-consuming and are not willing to commit many more hours every month to their "jobs." Even when teachers see this as part of their responsibility, they may have other concerns.

OVERCOMING THIS BARRIER   Teachers who do not believe that working with families is part of their job as teachers usually have not studied the issue of family involvement in their teacher training programs. Typically, when teachers realize the depth of the benefits of involving families in their child's education, they change their perceptions and are willing to try a few methods of communicating with families and sharing time with them.

Feeling Uncomfortable about Being Observed and Fear of Criticism

Teaching is, most often, an isolated profession. Other adults rarely watch as teachers work with students, so teachers become accustomed to being the only adult in the classroom. Because it is unusual for an adult to spend much time observing them, some teachers feel a bit uncomfortable when families are in the classroom. It is most likely the "newness" of the situation. But, when a parent comes in to observe them teaching, in addition to feeling uncomfortable, many teachers begin worrying about themselves and the students. They are concerned that the students' behavior and discussions will be different because of the presence of someone not usually in the classroom. They worry that the children will not "get" a concept and that it will make the teacher look like she doesn't know how to teach. They are anxious about the parent misinterpreting something they see in the classroom. All of this worry probably does affect the teacher's actions and conversations with students.

VOICES *of Teachers*

I hate it when parents drop into the classroom. Instantly this feeling comes over me. I question everything I am doing. Maybe I'm not teaching the right skills, and I just know that the parents will pick up on that. Or I think, "This room is so cluttered. Now this parent is going to think that I am disorganized." I worry about dozens of things, so much so that I have trouble continuing to teach when a parent walks in. Later, I can tell myself that I am a good teacher and that I shouldn't be afraid of parents. That's the intellectual side of my brain. But the next time a parent comes into the room, my emotions take over. I get caught up with worrying about everything and fearing that the parents will complain about me or how I teach.

Other teachers react more dramatically when an adult comes into their classroom. They become fearful. These teachers are afraid that the other adult—an administrator, another teacher, or a parent—is thinking negative things about them or their teaching and is there to criticize. Everyone worries about what to do when a parent, obviously in a bad mood, comes into the room or sends a complaint letter. But the fear of criticism can overwhelm some teachers. This occurs more often with first-year teachers, teachers who are not confident about their teaching practices, and teachers who do not feel very good about themselves in general.

OVERCOMING THIS BARRIER   If a particular situation makes someone feel uncomfortable, then the situation needs to be avoided or addressed. Most teachers do not want to avoid having parents in their classrooms, so feeling uncomfortable teaching while another adult is watching needs to be addressed. Most teachers find it less stressful to have friends watch them rather than the parents of a student. To overcome their discomfort, some teachers invite two or three friends to drop into the classroom and spend some time just observing. As they begin feeling more comfortable teaching around friends, they branch out to other adults. Over time, most teachers become relaxed enough to teach in front of any adult.

Uncertainty about How to Involve Family Members

Few of today's teachers grew up having family members volunteer in their own elementary school classrooms. Most teachers do not have a frame of reference for involving families in the life of the classroom. They feel that they have enough to do in planning learning experiences for students without having to plan for adults too. Instead of viewing volunteers as more resources to meet students' needs, they see adults in the classroom as just one more thing they have to plan for and monitor.

OVERCOMING THIS BARRIER The classroom teacher is the one who decides what family members will do in the classroom. Perhaps the easiest way to get families into the classroom is to ask them to join the class for a particular activity. It could be an end-of-the-day storytime, a set schedule for computer lab, a once-a-week block of time devoted to math games, or a reading workshop that occurs at the same time every day. Involving parents in learning experiences such as these would not require much time on the part of the

VOICES *of Teachers*

This is my first year to teach. I am barely surviving, trying to teach the way I learned to teach reading and writing and math and science and social studies and just keeping up with the schedule for lunch, computer lab, PE, and art. And, here I am in a school where parents volunteer a lot. I know I should be grateful, but in my college classes, no one talked about parents wanting to work in the classroom. I simply don't know what to do with those parents. I think it is kind of rude to ask them to make copies. I'm a little afraid to ask them to work with the children because I don't want them telling my students the way they used to do things in the old days, you know, things like "borrowing" to subtract or sounding out every word that the child doesn't know. And, I don't have time to tell parents how I teach math and reading. It is frustrating. I know it would be good to have more adults in the room, but I just can't figure out what to do with them.

teacher. At most, the teacher would need to spend a minute or two explaining to the adults how to support children's learning.

Another option is for the teacher to take a few minutes at the end of the day or during her lunchtime to explain to volunteers a particular classroom routine that they can help with. By outlining expectations to several people at the same time, the teacher doesn't feel she is "talking down" to the parents by explaining the ways things are done in her classroom. This is also reassuring to the parents who may be just as unsure about their responsibilities.

Summary

Although families and teachers generally support the idea of families being involved in the life of the classroom, the reality of actually having an active family involvement program is not easy to create. Families have reasons not to become involved. Teachers have concerns about letting families into their classrooms. However, teachers can overcome their own concerns and help families overcome barriers to their involvement. When the benefits are acknowledged and understood, both parties may be more willing to reach out to each other—and to the children.

Reflections

1. Put yourself in the position of a parent walking into your classroom for the first time. What would make you feel comfortable? How would you want the teacher to interact with you?
2. Consider comments you could make to help families feel comfortable in your classroom. Make a list of these statements and share them with another student.
3. Based on similar types of experiences, predict how you will feel when other adults observe you teaching, and make notes of things you could do to feel as relaxed as possible.

Field Experiences

1. Interview a first-year teacher and a veteran teacher about their feelings when parents come

into the class. What kinds of things did they do to overcome possible initial feelings of reluctance?
2. Interview families at different stages of parenthood (first child going to school, only child going to school, large family with all children in school, etc.). Ask about the reasons they are or are not involved in their child(ren)'s class.

Other Activities

1. Have a conversation among peers about concerns you may have about working with the families of students, and keep a list of these concerns. Trade lists with another group of peers, and brainstorm possible ways to overcome these concerns.
2. Reread "Issues of Time, Transportation, Child Care, and Other Logistical Problems." Select a center or school at random and research public transportation to that location.

Further Readings

Coleman, M. (1991). *Planning for parent participation in schools for young children.* ERIC Reproduction Document Number 3422463

It is important to build and maintain strong parent participation. Early childhood educators can plan parent participation by recognizing and overcoming barriers to participation, considering the resources and expertise of parents, developing communication strategies for such products as newsletters, planning ahead for parent–teacher conferences and following up on them, empowering parents with confidence, creating an environment that encourages information sharing, and limiting the number of educational objectives.

Lazar, A., & Slostad, F. (1999). How to overcome obstacles to parent-teacher partnerships. *Clearing House 72*, 206–210.

The authors review research about parent involvement. They discuss obstacles to parent–teacher collaboration, and contend that teachers need to rethink teacher–parent collaboration. Speaking to teachers, the authors argue that strong parent–teacher partnerships actually reduce the general level of stress associated with teaching.

Swick, K. J. (1992). *Teacher-parent partnerships.* ERIC Reproduction Document Number 351149

This article shares the parent and teacher attributes that support family–teacher partnerships and strategies that engage parents and teachers in collaborative roles, including home visits, conferences, parent centers, telecommunication, parent involvement in the classroom, participatory decision making, parent education programs, home learning activities, and family–school networking.

5

FAMILY

TEACHERS

COMMUNITY

Benefits of Family Involvement

Learning Objectives

The reader will learn and be able to discuss:

- The benefits of family involvement to children
- The benefits of family involvement to families
- The benefits of family involvement to teachers
- The benefits of family involvement to schools

The evidence is now beyond dispute.
When parents are involved in their children's education,
their children do better in school.

—Anne Henderson and Nancy Berla, 1995

The positive effects of teachers and families working together are well documented. In fact, a family's involvement in their children's education is held in such high regard that the National Education Goals Panel (1998) included the enhancement of parental participation among its list of goals for the nation's schools. When teachers and families work together, both of them benefit from the process. However, the people who benefit most from an effective working relationship between teachers and families are the children.

Benefits to Children

Research indicates that children benefit significantly when their families are involved in their education. These benefits range from school success as measured through grades and standardized test scores (Epstein, 1991; Fan and Chen, 1999; Stevenson and Baker, 1987) to smaller school issues such as day-to-day attendance and enrollment in higher academic programs (Trusty, 1999; Yonezawa, 2000) to higher levels of social skills such as behavior in school, motivation, and interactions with teachers and with peers (Palenchar, Vondra, and Wilson, 2001; Sanders, 1998).

Children generally experience positive feelings when their mothers, fathers, or other family members come to school to join in learning experiences. The child in the box below expresses her feelings in words typical of a kindergarten child. She "likes" it when her mother comes to school. But, the benefits children experience when their teacher and family work together are much more significant than just happy feelings.

VOICES *of Children*

I like it when my mom comes to my school. Sometimes she comes and eats lunch with me. Sometimes she comes at story time and I get to sit beside her.

Success in School

Perhaps the most important benefit of family involvement to children is increased school success and higher academic achievement (Epstein, 1991; Fan and Chen, 1999; Stevenson and Baker, 1987). Recent research studies have shown specific positive impact on student success in learning reading and mathematics skills (Faires et al., 2000; Chavkin and Gonzalez, 2000; Quigley, 2000) and in other content areas such as language arts, literacy, art, science, and social

Parents learn about the class when they join class meetings.

studies (Bloome et al., 2000; Epstein et al., 2003). These research studies demonstrate a positive correlation between family involvement and student achievement in just about every academic area studied in the elementary school.

Regardless of socioeconomic status, ethnic or racial background, or the parents' education level, students achieve more when their parents are involved in their education. The more extensive the parent involvement is, the higher the student achievement rises (Henderson and Berla, 1995). Among the factors that lead to this improved achievement is the fact that when parents are involved in their child's school, they are more likely to talk to children about school. They monitor their children's schoolwork more frequently and in more detail. They work more on helping their children learn when they receive information from teachers about classroom learning activities, their child's strength and progress, and specific suggestions about how to help children learn (Epstein, 2001).

Henderson and Berla's survey of research on family involvement (1995) also identified several other benefits to children:

"In programs that are designed to involve parents in full partnerships, student achievement for disadvantaged children not only improves, it can reach levels

that are standard for middle-class children. In addition, the children who are farthest behind make the greatest gains.

Children from diverse cultural backgrounds tend to do better when parents and professionals collaborate to bridge the gap between the culture at home and the learning institution.

The benefits of involving parents are not confined to the early years; there are significant gains at all ages and grade levels.

The most accurate predictor of a student's achievement in school is not income or social status, but the extent to which that student's family is able to (1) create a home environment that encourages learning; (2) communicate high, yet reasonable, expectations for their children's achievement and future careers; and (3) become involved in their children's education at school and in the community (www.pta.org/programs).

The research is clear. When teachers and families work together, the children are more successful in school. Some of this increased success can be explained simply by the increased time that children spend thinking about and working on school-related issues. When families reinforce the learning that is happening at school, children learn more and remember it for longer periods of time.

Additionally, when teachers and families work together, they most likely share more information about the child. Each observes the child in different settings, so together they can put together a more complete picture of the child than either could do alone (Gestwicki, 2000).

Benefits for Siblings

When a family gets involved in the education of one of their children, the other children in the family benefit. Research on Head Start programs demonstrated that when families were involved in the Head Start program, siblings of the child enrolled in the program benefited. The child who attended the Head Start program and his or her siblings showed an increase in IQ score while in the program. Both the child and the siblings retained these IQ gains (Schweinhart and Weikart, 1986).

Beyond IQ gains, families who are active in one child's education learn parenting strategies that help them be better parents for their other children. Recent studies suggest that the earliest years in a child's life are the most important ones. During these first few years, parents are the child's first, and primary, teacher. Parents' actions and interactions with the child support or deter the child's cognitive, social, emotional, and physical development. Beyond

VOICES *of Children*

My mom helps me at night. My teacher sends home notes about what we are doing at school. My mom reads the notes and she knows how to help me learn more. I like it when my mom knows what we are studying and helps me, so the next day, I know more.

VOICES of Administrators

From an administrator's perspective, I cannot emphasize the importance of family involvement enough. The more parents know about what goes on in their child's class, the better they are able to work with their child in ways that support and extend what the children are learning at school. The research is clear. A good classroom teacher and parents' involvement in their child's education creates the strongest possible learning environment for a child.

So I do anything I can do to support family involvement. I work closely with the PTA to get more family members in the school, for meetings or for volunteering, but that is not enough, in my opinion.

I don't have any research to back up this belief about family involvement, but I think the classroom teachers are in a position to involve more families than anyone else in the schools. Parents are more likely to get involved when teachers are reaching out to families, sending home lots of information about what is happening in their classes, inviting parents to school for all kinds of class activities, and just making sure that all parents know that we have an open-door policy at our school.

Parents tend to be more willing to come to meetings led by their child's teacher than they are to meetings that I lead or that another parent leads. They are more interested when their teacher is talking about their class.

So I have worked over the past five or six years to include some money in our school budget to support teachers' hosting meetings with the families of their students. It is not much, but it pays for a sitter for children so the adults can meet together without the interruption of young children, and it pays for some snacks. I will keep working to increase this budget line because I strongly believe that increased family involvement, and all the things that leads to, is worth the investment of some of the school's money.

that, parents' actions and interactions with the child physiologically wire the brain.

Many parents are unaware of how important the first three years of life are or what types of experiences they should provide for their infants and toddlers for maximum support of development, including brain development. Family involvement programs at the school level often provide information about child development and strategies for interacting appropriately with children. When this knowledge changes a parent's behaviors at home, all the children in the home benefit from the more appropriate interactions. Early childhood educators at the class level share with families activities and experiences that help young children learn. When families implement these teaching strategies for one child, other children in the family are typically nearby, so the siblings benefit as well.

Benefits to Families

Families also benefit from being involved in their child's education. Involved families generally have a more positive attitude about schools and teachers (Bauch, 2001; Sanders, Epstein, and Connors-Tadros, 1999). When comparing groups of families who were actively involved in school to groups of families who were not involved at all, Epstein (1996) found that the involved families were "significantly more likely than other parents to feel they received many ideas of how to help their children at home, to believe that they understood more about their child's curriculum, and to feel more positively about the teacher's interpersonal skills and teaching ability" (pp. 10–11).

Knowledge of School/Class

When parents spend time in the classroom or attend informational meetings with the classroom teacher, they learn specifics about how the class is organized and which instructional strategies the teacher uses on a regular basis. Knowing how the classroom is arranged, what the general daily schedule is, and some of the routines that the class follows helps parents understand more about their child's education. Further, it helps parents have more meaningful conversations about school with

VOICES *of Families*

I have come to depend on my child's teacher. She sends home notes every week about the kinds of things they are doing in the class. That way I know exactly what to do to help my son. With my other children, I read to them and listened to them read to me, but that was about all I knew to do. This teacher lets me know that they are working on certain skills and gives suggestions on how to help at home. I do those things she suggests. Now, I feel like I am really helping my child.

their children. Parents can go beyond the typical "how was your day?" or "what did you do at school today" kinds of conversations.

Knowledge about Children

By being involved in their child's class, families also learn about child development issues. Through interactions with teachers, they benefit from the knowledge teachers gain during their early childhood education training and what they continue to learn by staying current on research relating to young children's learning. Many families come to depend on teachers for advice about parenting issues not only for the child in that teacher's class, but for siblings as well. Teachers of young children learn very specialized knowledge about young children as they prepare to become a teacher. They learn the principles of child growth and development. They are also trained in ways that children learn best, how to teach to children's strengths, how to support children in areas that need strengthening, and how to guide children and foster positive behavior. After completing college courses, early childhood educators continue learning about young children through personal reading and multiple professional development opportunities. In addition to formal study, teachers also gain significant knowledge about children through their practical experiences working with all kinds of children. Families can benefit from this

Teachers welcome the families of their students into the class.

knowledge about young children and skills in working with them through informal conversations or simply through observing teachers as they teach. What families learn from teachers can be used as they parent their own children.

Parenting Support

Some families rely on teachers for more than casual sharing of information. In previous generations, new parents relied on their own parents or other close relatives for advice about parenting. With the mobility of today's society, many families do not have this resource. They often turn to early childhood educators for the advice and support they would typically ask of their own family.

Parents may also benefit from informal connections they make with members of other families. When family members spend time at school attending school-level or class-level meetings or volunteering, they are likely to interact with other adults.

VOICES *of Families*

I owe a lot to my son's kindergarten teacher. I have always been a shy person. I don't feel comfortable being around groups of people, so I have never been much of a joiner. One afternoon when I was picking up Kyle from school, Mrs. Williams asked me if I would consider coming into the class once a week to work with a group of five children in some kind of reading activity. At first I was reluctant, but I couldn't think of a good excuse fast enough, so I found myself saying yes. I showed up every Friday just after their lunch and I helped the children in some kind of literature extension activity. We did all kinds of things. We cooked stone soup after reading that book. We painted a huge mural after reading a book about dinosaurs. We made help-wanted posters after reading *Chicken Little* by Stephen Kellogg. I really started looking forward to those Fridays. Then Mrs. Williams asked if I would come to a family meeting and talk about what I was doing with the children. Reluctantly, I agreed, but had a good time when I was talking with the parents. From that meeting on, I attended all of Mrs. Williams' family meetings. In those meetings, she talked about what was happening in the class, but we also talked about our children at home—you know, things like getting kids to eat balanced meals and getting them to bed at a reasonable hour. I discovered that almost every other parent had the same problems that I thought only I had. It felt good to realize I wasn't really a bad mother. From those conversations in family meetings, I even found myself making friends among other parents. I think back now to the beginning of the school year. I am involved in a group of people now and have more friends all because I said yes to my son's teacher when she asked if I would help her do something good for children.

They automatically have something in common—that their children attend the same school—so friendships or other helping relationships are often a result of meeting other adults at school (Swap, 1993).

Adult Education

Some schools offer adult education classes, such as English as a second language, different computer programs, and parenting classes. Parents who are already involved in the school in some way tend to enroll in these classes because they feel comfortable at the school. When these classes are available, this is another benefit to families as a result of their involvement in school.

Benefits to Teachers

If only children and their families benefited from family involvement in the class, the investment of a teacher's time would be worth it. However, that is not the case. Teachers also benefit from family involvement.

Teaching is often an isolating experience. One benefit of family involvement is the reduction of this isolation. The teacher is still responsible for all educational decisions and curriculum planning, but having other adults in the classroom offers opportunities for collaboration.

Less Isolation

Research (Henderson and Berla, 1995) indicates that strong family involvement leads to improved teacher morale, higher ratings of teachers by parents, and a better reputation of the school in the community. When parents recognize the complexity of a teacher's roles, there is a sense of comfort for teachers in that acknowledgment (Swap, 1993). This recognition from parents helps teachers move away from the feelings that "I am in this alone," and "No one appreciates all that I do."

More Effective Teaching

Just as families can learn about their children from teachers, teachers can learn information from families that makes them more effective in their work with individual children. Typically, the closer the relationship between the teacher and families, the more information the family is willing to share. Sudden changes in a child's behavior might be mystifying to a teacher. However, those changes would be totally understandable if a family member shared information about a particularly stressful event in the child's life. These stressful events include an illness or death in the immediate or extended family, the loss of a job, an impending move, or any number of other events that might upset a young child.

More Resources

When families are involved in the life of the class, the teacher benefits from having more resources—both people and things—in the classroom. With more adults in the room, the teacher can offer more to the students. Organized, but active, small group activities such as cooking, gardening, or woodworking run more smoothly when several adults are in the room to support children's work.

Benefits to Schools

Beyond benefiting children, families, and teachers, family involvement also affects the schools as organizations. When families are actively involved in schools, they can affect the school climate in a positive way, even leading to a more open school culture. This finding was particularly true for a study of schools organized by the Comer model and Zigler's schools of the twenty-first century (Jordan, Orozco, and

VOICES *of Teachers*

It was my first year of teaching, so I had no experience to fall back on. In college classes, I had learned about the importance of working with families, but during field experiences, I had heard that teachers could not depend on families in high-poverty areas for any kind of involvement in the classroom. Not sure what would happen, I started out the year with letters to families and a family meeting and just trusted that things would work out. Three mothers in that class kind of adopted me. They were always bringing me food, insisting that I needed to eat better. They would bring me salads for lunch or vegetables that I just had to warm up for dinner. Whenever I asked for volunteers to do some kind of special activity with the class, they were there. After a couple of months when we got to know each other pretty well, they realized how much money I was spending on the classroom. They didn't have a lot of discretionary income to buy things I needed, but they insisted that I write out a list of the things I wanted for my classroom. They would shop garage sales and find things for me for very little money. I bought fabric and they sewed curtains for the classroom. The night before Public School Night, one mother watched all the children and the other two mothers worked with me in the classroom from 4:00 until almost 10:00 painting the walls so the room would not look so dreary. Those mothers gave me so much support that first year. I don't know how I would have made it that first year without them.

Averett, 2002). Studies also show that family involvement influences school reform efforts in a positive way (Desimone et al., 2000). Parents tend to play one or more of three roles in school reform efforts. They actually participate in the reform efforts in the school their children attend, act as full partners in the reform efforts, or serve as reform advocates.

Summary

Family involvement may be defined in many different ways, but research demonstrates that when families get involved in their child's education and involved in schools, everyone in the process benefits. The school as an organization benefits. Adults, family members and teachers, benefit. But, most of all, and perhaps most importantly, children benefit.

Reflections

1. Think back to your own elementary school days. Was your family involved in your classes? If they were, how did that make you feel? If they were not, how do you think you might have felt if they had been involved?
2. With the benefits of family involvement to children so clear, how might you share this information in ways that would change the thinking and practices of families and/or teachers?

Field Experiences

1. Identify a teacher who considers family involvement a priority. Interview her about how she believes she personally benefits from families' involvement in her class.
2. Identify two parents of different children who are active in their child's class. Interview them separately about the reasons for their involvement and how they think they benefit personally from this involvement.

Other Activities

1. Create a pamphlet detailing the benefits to families of their involvement in their children's school.

Share the pamphlet with two families and get their feedback. Ask if being aware of these benefits might change what they do with their children and their schools.

2. Create a brochure for teachers that details the benefits of family involvement to teachers. Include the benefits to children and families as well. Share the brochure with practicing teachers and get their feedback. Compare the pamphlet and the brochure to note their differences based on the main audience for the two pieces.

Further Readings

Henderson, A., & Berla, N. (1995). *A new generation of evidence: The family is critical to student achievement.* Washington, DC: Center for Law and Education.

Henderson and Berla make research about family involvement accessible to all readers. They provide solid evidence that quality family involvement is needed for children to succeed and that the highest gains come from more substantial involvement.

Jones, R. (2001). Involving parents is a whole new game: Be sure you win! *Education Digest, 67*(3), 36–44.

This article suggests ways to involve parents that boost student achievement.

Website to Explore

■ Hand in Hand: Parents Schools Communities United for Kids
www.handinhand.org

6

FAMILY

TEACHERS

COMMUNITY

Written Communication

Learning Objectives

The reader will learn and be able to discuss:

- Ways that teachers can communicate with families in writing
- Ways that schools can communicate with families in writing

I always receive positive responses from parents when my letters are personal and chock-full of examples and newsworthy bits of information.

—Shelley Harwayne, 1999

Virtually all early childhood programs send some kind of written communication home to families. Some publish handbooks. Others create newsletters. All send home reminder notes about upcoming events. Writing is probably the most time-efficient way of conveying information to families. However, early childhood educators remember that not all families respond to the same type of written communication. So, both teachers and administrators look for various ways of sharing "news" that meet the needs of different families. Some forms of written communication are effective for classroom teachers, and some seem to be more effective when used at the school level.

Classroom Level

Even when the school or center sends information to families, it does not take the place of written information from the classroom teacher. Newsletters or notices from the school are typically about procedures or general information for everyone involved in the school. The classroom teacher has different information to share with families: stories about the class where their children spend every school day, specific topics that class is exploring, and books they are reading. Families want to hear about their children, how they spend their days, and what they are learning. Letters from administrators rarely give this kind of information. So classroom teachers balance what families want with how much time they have to devote to this type of communication. There are several ways to communicate in writing with family members:

- ☑ Weekly letters
- ☑ Weekly newsletters
- ☑ Suggested activities that support school learning
- ☑ Individual notes
- ☑ Student-created newsletters
- ☑ Two-way communication

Teachers use those methods that work best for them and the families in the lives of their students.

Letters of Introduction

Written communication can begin even before the school year does. Sensitive teachers recognize that many families feel anxious just before the school starts. They are filled with questions: Who will my child's teacher be? What kind of person

Teachers write notes to children.

is she? Will she like my child? Will she understand my child? All of these questions are normal. After all, families are turning over their children to a virtual stranger for six or seven hours a day for an entire school year.

Teachers can help address this anxiety by communicating with the families before the school year starts. Teachers send a letter of introduction to the family, much like the sample in Box 6.1. Families will form initial impressions of their child's teacher from the tone and the content of a letter of introduction. Since it is important to come across as a warm, open person who cares about young children and their families, it is important to spend extra time crafting a letter that reflects your personality and conveys your respect of young children.

Some teachers also include a personal note to each new student in the letter of introduction or mail notes to students separately. These notes do not have to be long. The sample note in Box 6.2 takes less than three minutes to write. It is a small investment of time, but children love receiving their very own mail and will feel like they are important to their "new" teacher.

TIP

Reading a family letter aloud to yourself is a good way to check the tone of the letter and to catch awkward phrasing and typographical errors. Additionally, it never hurts to ask a friend to proof the letter. You want that first letter to leave a good impression with families.

BOX 6.1 | *Letter of Introduction to Families*

Dear Families,

The new school year begins in less than two weeks. Your child will be in my first-grade class, so we will be working together for the next ten months. I thought I would let you know a little bit about myself and what you can expect during the first few weeks of school.

This is my thirteenth year of teaching either prekindergarten, kindergarten, or first grade. For me, there is something special about teaching young children. At this age, they are such curious, energetic, and enthusiastic learners.

I believe that young children learn best when they are active. When you walk into our classroom, you'll notice that the room is arranged by learning centers. Much of our day will be spent working in the art, dramatic play, listening, math, reading, sand, science, and writing centers. A good question to ask your child at the end of a school day is, "What center did you work in today?" Remember, it's never a good idea to ask, "What did you do today?" because most 5-year-olds have one of two answers to that question: "play" or "nothing." Neither answer is very satisfying for you.

You'll also notice that the classroom seems a little bare. The learning centers are arranged, but little else has been done to the room. I've done that on purpose. I want the children to feel a real sense of ownership of the room, so during the first week of school, we will work together to create bulletin boards, write class labels, and add materials to each center.

I am married with one teenage son. We used to do things as a family all the time. My son now prefers friends over parents. So I spend most of my free time reading about teaching while running a taxi service and a 24-hour restaurant for my son and his friends. This note tells you a little about me.

I would like to know more about your family. I know my teaching must begin with making your child feel comfortable at school and in our class. Would you please take a quiet moment to write whatever you think would help me get to know you and your child? These questions could guide your thinking: What is your child like? When he or she is upset, how do you comfort him or her? What are your child's interests and your family's interests? Thanks for taking the time to write to me. I believe that sharing information will help us all get to know each other. I am looking forward to this year and the opportunities we will all create for the children in our classroom.

Sincerely,

BOX 6.2 | *Letter of Introduction to Child*

August 5

Dear Darriell,

You are going to be in
my class this year. I am
so happy. I can't wait to
meet you. We are going to
learn a lot of things and
have so much fun in kindergarten.

I'll see you soon.

Mrs. Johnson

Weekly Letters

Weekly letters are one way early childhood educators keep families informed about the life of the classroom. The format and content of these letters are as varied as the teachers who write them. However, in weekly letters, most teachers give a summary of what has happened in the classroom that week, let families know some of the topics the class is studying, and offer suggestions for ways that families can support children's learning. The letter might read something like the one in Box 6.3.

In addition to the letter itself, the teacher might include other information:

☑ Copies of poems, songs, or fingerplays the children learned
☑ Titles of books that were read aloud that week
☑ Directions for a math game the children learned

BOX 6.3 | *Weekly Letter*

Dear Families:

As always, this week has been filled with lots of activity and learning. On Monday, a long-haired guinea pig came to live in our science center. The children voted to name her Popsicle. We've spent quite a bit of time reading about guinea pigs. We've observed her and made daily entries in our science observation logs. We have compared what we know about gerbils with what we are learning about guinea pigs. I am helping the children focus on how the animals are the same and how they are different. If you have a chance to come into the classroom, you can see the chart we are working on. Your child may refer to the chart as a graphic organizer or a Venn diagram. It looks something like this:

Only Gerbils	The Same	Only Guinea Pigs

Your child can answer questions about what we've written on the chart or about what Popsicle likes to eat, how she gets water, and where she lives.

We are continuing to work on adding numbers up to 20. In class, the children usually use Unifix® cubes to make the numbers more concrete. Once they have 10 cubes in the 1s place, they snap them together and move them to the left into the 10s place. You can borrow Unifix cubes from the classroom or just use any concrete item around the house to practice adding. When you work on addition, remember to pose problems to your child that relate to his or her life: cookies they share with a brother, pieces of fruit to give to the rodents in the science center, or marbles to play a game with a friend.

Our author of the week was Tomie de Paola. His books seem to be in every center in the classroom. I'm not sure how many books de Paola has written, but we have 39 in the room right now and are still looking for others. You may hear comments from your child such as, "Real artists don't copy," "He doesn't pay attention," and "Arruga." These come from some of de Paola's books (*The Art Lesson, Strega Nona,* and *Tom*). If you get a chance to go to the library, I'm sure you'll enjoy any of the de Paola books you can check out.

We will still be reading de Paola books next week at the end of the day. If you can come by the school a bit early, we would love to share our story time with you.

Sincerely,

VOICES *of Families*

I have three children, one in kindergarten, one in middle school, and one in high school. My youngest daughter's kindergarten teacher is the first teacher who has ever asked me about my child. I was so impressed. This teacher actually acknowledged that I know things about my child that would help her be a better teacher for Drew. The letter she sent us was a small gesture. I mean, it didn't take her very long to write that letter telling us about herself and asking about us, but it meant so much to my husband and me. I think this may be a very different year, working with a teacher like this.

- ☑ Reminders to families about upcoming topics of study or special events
- ☑ Suggested activities for families and children to share
- ☑ Articles from a parenting magazine

Placing the weekly letter and other information together in a pocket folder increases the chance that the information will make it home intact.

Letters like the one in Box 6.3 serve several purposes. In addition to keeping families informed about the class, these letters can help educate families. The teacher can use weekly letters to share teaching strategies being used in the class, ways that young children learn best, or the learning that is embedded in classroom activities that may look like "just playing" to those not familiar with current early childhood practice.

Time is always an issue for early childhood educators. For some topics, a teacher might include a

Children can be responsible for assembling weekly folders of information to send home.

TIP

Teachers need to consider their audience and write at a level that most families of students can read and comprehend. Not all families are literate, and many do not read English. For illiterate families, the teacher can audiotape the weekly letter and send home the audiotape with a small hand-held cassette player. Audiotapes can be duplicated fairly easily with a recorder that has a double cassette. For families who do not read English or understand oral English, volunteers can be recruited to translate the teacher's weekly letters onto audiotapes.

copy of a journal article and just reference the article in the letter. For other topics, short explanations found in books such as *Family Friendly Communication in Early Childhood Programs* (Diffily and Morrison, 1997) can be copied and sent home. The *Family Friendly Communication* article about the learning involved in the block center is in Box 6.4.

Weekly letters remind families that the teacher is reaching out to them. With the consistency of a letter being sent home every week, families realize that the teacher truly cares about keeping them informed. They come to believe that the teacher is just as concerned about them as she is about the children. Family members who feel that they are valued by teachers are much more likely to become involved in the life of the class.

Invitations to join the class for specific activities are often included in weekly letters. In the sample letter in Box 6.4, the teacher offers two informal invitations for family members to come to the class: first, to look at the Venn diagram the class is creating and second, to join the class for an end-of-the-day story time. This shows that the teacher is not only willing for families to come into the classroom, but she is arranging specific opportunities for them. Not all families will respond positively to weekly letters or informal invitations to come into the classroom, but many will. It is important to remember that not all parents will respond to one particular type of written communication.

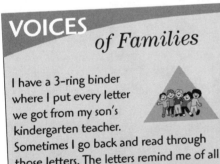

VOICES *of Families*

I have a 3-ring binder where I put every letter we got from my son's kindergarten teacher. Sometimes I go back and read through those letters. The letters remind me of all the things they did in his class, from pictures they painted to books they read to science experiments they did. I can't imagine a better way to remember his first year in school.

Suggested Activities that Support School Learning

By investing only two or three hours a month, teachers can generate dozens of activities for children and families to work on together at home. Often families want to help but are not sure how to best support their children's learning. Sending home age-appropriate activities that are related to classroom learning experiences provides guidance for families and extends children's learning at home.

Many types of activities are appropriate for children and their families:

BOX 6.4 | *Learning with Blocks*

Blocks are open-ended materials that stimulate young imaginations, provide choices for discovery and invention, and promote the development of problem-solving skills. One day a block may be an airplane. The next day that same block in the hands of the same child can be a sofa for the house he is building.

Building with blocks helps develop young children's eye–hand coordination, visual perception, and large and small motor skills. It builds self-confidence and provides opportunities for creativity and dramatic play. These things occur naturally when children play with blocks.

We also find that working with blocks often deepens children's engagement with literature and literacy. A child may be inspired, say, to construct the three bears' beds and chairs, a pirate boat, or an enchanted castle.

We sometimes take photographs of children's block creations and invite the children to caption the photos. We also encourage girls and boys to make their own signs for their creations. In these activities, children are exposed to print in meaningful ways.

Inviting children to reconstruct buildings and other things they have seen on field trips is one way we encourage their thinking in relation to social studies. They work with the concepts behind maps and models, and as they build block cities, farms, and factories, they work out their own understanding of these complex sites and communities. Children also develop mathematical and scientific concepts, such as balance and gravity, as they work with blocks.

Blocks are engrossing and fun for young children, of course. They are also invaluable tools for promoting children's development on many fronts.

TIP

Sending the weekly letter home on the same day of the week helps families know when to expect the letter. Some teachers always copy the letter onto the same shade of colored paper, so that the letter stands out from other papers in the child's folder. Other teachers create "class stationery" and use this for their weekly letters. (See Box 6.5)

☑ Reading books and completing literature responses
☑ Writing dialogue journals
☑ Playing word games
☑ Playing math games
☑ Following recipes
☑ Conducting simple science experiences

Individual Notes

Informal notes are often used to let individual families know something about their child. All too often, teachers use these notes to communicate a negative incident that occurred at school. Although negative notes are necessary at times, it is equally important that families hear positive things about their child. It

BOX 6.5 | *A Sample of Class Stationery*

BOX 6.6 | *Suggested Activities for Families and Children to Share*

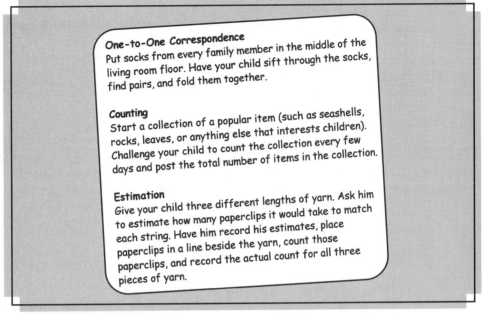

One-to-One Correspondence
Put socks from every family member in the middle of the living room floor. Have your child sift through the socks, find pairs, and fold them together.

Counting
Start a collection of a popular item (such as seashells, rocks, leaves, or anything else that interests children). Challenge your child to count the collection every few days and post the total number of items in the collection.

Estimation
Give your child three different lengths of yarn. Ask him to estimate how many paperclips it would take to match each string. Have him record his estimates, place paperclips in a line beside the yarn, count those paperclips, and record the actual count for all three pieces of yarn.

takes only a couple of minutes to jot a quick note about a child's act of kindness, a cute comment he or she made, or a milestone in learning. Just as weekly letters let families know you are concerned about keeping them informed, notes to families let them know that you carefully observe your students and that you value their children.

Notes are not always sent to the child's family. They can be given directly to the child or many teachers slip notes of appreciation or pride into a child's folder. These notes are very specific. By the time young children get home from school, they may not remember what they did to deserve a generic note of appreciation. A note with the printed statement "_____ was a super helper today," may not mean anything to the child or to the child's family. When notes are more specific, they are meaningful to the child and to the family. Notes can be as simple as two or three sentences.

- ✓ Today, I noticed you let Andre paint at the easel before you. Thank you for being a kind friend to Andre.
- ✓ At lunch I heard Josie ask for one of your cookies. It is not always easy to let someone have part of your dessert. Thank you for sharing.
- ✓ Today when Sheneka spilled the pattern blocks, I saw you leave the reading center and help her pick up every single one of those blocks. I appreciate it when you help other children.
- ✓ I know that you have been struggling with writing the sounds in words you wanted to write. Today I heard you stretching the words and writing the letters that make those sounds. You are working hard!

TIP

Because teachers are likely to jot notes at odd times—during lunch, recess, or self-selected center time—it is a good idea to keep a checklist of how many notes have been sent to each child. While it is not necessary to send exactly the same number of notes to each child, there should be some equity. A checklist helps ensure that no child is inadvertently overlooked.

These notes can be written on a simple piece of stationery, brightly colored plain paper, or a variety of clip-art forms. It matters less what type of paper is used than the fact that you are taking a few minutes out of the day to let children and families know that you notice specific acts and appreciate them.

Student-Created Newsletters

There are few pieces sent from school that families enjoy reading more than information written and produced by their own children. Student-created newsletters could be something as simple as a preprinted form. Before children's writing becomes readable by other adults, the teacher can take dictation from children about their activities of the week or even of the day.

BOX 6.7 | *News of the Day Sample*

Day Monday

Date October 17

Jordan said, "Today we had hamburgers for lunch."

Travis told the class, "I am going to my grandma's house tonight."

Deidra said, "I did Kid Pix at the computer."

Michael said, "My dad is picking me up today."

TIP

News of the Day

Many early childhood educators have an end-of-the-day ritual. Standing near an overhead projector, they transcribe children's dictations about their day. The class rereads each sentence after dictation, then choral reads the entire page. The teacher creates brief lessons about writing based on what the children have dictated. Then the teacher copies one for each child in the class and sends them home. Over time, children use these "News of the Day" sheets for at-home reading practice. This ritual covers two important areas: informing families and reading instruction/practice.

When children's writing develops to the point that their developmental spelling can be read by most adults, children can write their own entries for the newsletter. Then they can literally cut and paste their articles into a newsletter-looking product. Also, children can use numerous computer programs to create simple newsletters. These can be shared as printed copies or posted on a website to be read electronically. Other ways children can share information are to create invitations, fliers, brochures, announcements, and so on.

Two-Way Communication

Notes to individual families can be written on any type of paper; however, these are one-way communication, from the teacher to the family. Changing the type of paper used to write notes can change the communication into a two-way exchange. Stapling together several pieces of notebook paper, putting them into a pocket folder, and attaching a note such as the one in Box 6.8 gives the teacher readily available paper for notes. At the same time, it invites families to write to the teacher.

Even young children can work on parts of a class newsletter to send home.

BOX 6.8 | *Invitation to Write to Teacher*

Dear Families,

I would like us to communicate often. The notebook paper in this folder is for us to write notes back and forth. From time to time, I'll write a note to you about your child, and I hope you'll write to me. You can also use this paper for any questions you have. I'll answer questions as quickly as possible. Let's work together to make this a wonderful year for your child.

Deborah

Although it is not necessary for a classroom teacher to use each of these methods of written communication to families, it may be a good idea to experiment with two or three methods. Not all families respond in the same way to weekly letters, regular newsletters, suggested activities that support school learning, individual notes, student-created newsletters, or two-way communication. The teacher should choose those methods that work best for her and the families of her students.

Email

Not all families have access to email, but for those who do, this is a time-efficient way of communicating with families. Handwriting a note to families is a typical way of communicating with individual families, but writing a note takes more time than typing it, and a teacher can never be sure that the child actually delivers the note to the parents. Email is created more quickly and almost always gets to the intended family member whether they are at home, at work, or out of town. Email can also be used in place of weekly letters and notes of reminder about any number of events.

School Level

Teachers should not be responsible for all communication that is sent home to families. While teachers write about the students and the life of one classroom, there are many issues that affect all families in the school. If for nothing other than consistency, this type of communication should be produced by the administration.

Orientation Packet

An orientation packet could include any number of written materials that would help families understand the school or center better. Often a letter from the principal or center director is the first item that is seen when opening the orientation packet. This letter expresses appreciation for a family's interest in the school and provides a few key points about the school. Brochures describing the school's philosophy, a history of the school, and special services of the school (parent resource library, parenting classes, before-school and after-school child care programs, special enrichment classes for children, etc.) are included in the packet. Some schools also include copies of newspaper articles about the school or magazine articles that describe some of the school's philosophies. On the more practical side, all forms associated with enrollment are put into this packet: application forms, forms about contact information, and forms about a child's background and interests. The orientation packet offers sufficient information so that families and other interested parties get a good feel for the school.

Family Handbook

The audience for an orientation packet is fairly broad, but the audience for a family handbook is much more specific. A family handbook is meant for the parents and other caregivers of the children attending a particular school or center. A handbook is an efficient way to communicate the school's philosophy, basic information about the school, policies and procedures, and general information. Having this information in one place and available to all families helps eliminate misunderstandings. The following issues are commonly included in a handbook.

VOICES *of Teachers*

Whenever I stop and think how I used to communicate with families, I am so grateful for today's technology. I used to spend at least 30 minutes a day writing notes to send home. It was important to me to let each family know how their child was doing, so I would write two or three notes every day. Now I can send the same number of notes in a third of the time. And, having a website lets parents see so much more of our class and what we do than I ever could share with them five years ago. In addition to written explanations that I used to send home, I have photographs so family members can really see into the classroom. Technology is great.

SCHOOL PHILOSOPHY The educational philosophy that guides the school often leads the family handbook. Many schools have a mission statement which certainly can be included in the handbook, but mission statements tend to be brief. There needs to be an expanded explanation of the school's philosophy and how the philosophy affects the day-to-day educational life of children: why rooms are arranged the way they are, what kinds of learning experiences are provided for different ages of children, how teachers interact with children, and other similar issues.

BASIC INFORMATION ABOUT THE SCHOOL Basic information about the school includes the name of the school, the address, and telephone number (email and website addresses, if available). A calendar of school days and holidays is included, as well as the hours that the school or center is open. Employees' names and titles are often listed under the category of basic information.

SCHOOL POLICIES School policies cover a number of topics. One area of policy addresses the issue of children's illness. Schools have different policies about when children may come to school and when they should be kept at home (e.g. children must be free of temperature for 24 hours before returning to school). Time-tables are given to families, related to how long children should be kept at home when they have had diseases such as chicken pox, the flu, or even the common cold.

Discipline or guidance issues are typically a major concern for families. It is not possible to list every possible situation and relate how it would be handled. But it is important that families understand the general approach to discipline, whether it is behavior modification and a reward system or is a longer-term approach to the development of self-control within a community of learners. It is important that all families understand how adults in the school or center respond to day-to-day issues related to children's behavior.

Other policy issues include how the progress of a child is reported to families, if and when conferences are held, how family involvement is permitted or encouraged, and the procedures families should use to resolve problems they perceive.

> **TIP**
>
> **Publishing a Family Handbook**
>
> Most schools and centers keep the text of the handbook on disk, so they can more easily revise or update it each year. The handbook can simply be printed, copied, and stapled or spiral bound. Volunteers can bind a sufficient number of copies in a few hours.

School Newsletter

Different schools produce different types of newsletters. In some schools, the principal or director has sole responsibility for the content of the newsletter. At other schools, a general format is agreed to at the beginning of the school year, and different people write different "columns" for each newsletter.

A standard format can be created through the use of columns, boxed information, white space, logo/clip art/graphics, and varied fonts and sizes. These varied features give a newsletter an informal, reader-friendly look. Before writing the first school newsletter, the person in charge of compiling it determines the primary purposes of the newsletter. There are several purposes for a school newsletter:

☑ Keeping parents informed about classroom activities
☑ Providing insight into the educational purposes of classroom activities
☑ Educating parents with information on child development
☑ Acting as a "clearinghouse" for parenting books, videos, parent education classes, and events in the community designed to appeal to families
☑ Assisting in the recruitment of volunteer help
☑ Acknowledging donations of time, materials, and money (Rockwell, Andre, and Hawley, 1995, p. 126)

Once the purpose(s) of the newsletter has been determined, it is a good idea to decide on columns that will appear in every issue. When families know that they will find regular features, they come to anticipate those and look forward to reading certain columns. When the newsletter format is inviting and the text is informative, most families will at least skim the school newsletter.

Family Surveys

Orientation packets, family handbooks, and school newsletters are one-way communication from the school to the families. Just as it is important for the classroom teacher to encourage two-way communication, it is also important for administrators to encourage families to communicate with the school. Families' voices need to be heard by administration, teachers, and staff.

One of the easier ways for administrators to solicit families' opinions is to distribute surveys or questionnaires. A principal or center director can create a simple survey about a specific topic as a quick way to get an understanding about how families feel about that topic. It could be something as simple as selecting a date for an all-school meeting and trying to find a date that would accommodate the most number of people. It could be something as complicated as decision making about how surplus funds in the budget should be spent.

 Summary

Written communication plays an important role in building relationships between the school and families associated with the school. Classroom teachers play an important role in sharing information about children and their classrooms. Administration shares information important to everyone in the school community. Both teachers and administrators have many options about communicating information to families. Each group considers their audiences and chooses communication methods that work best for them and the families with whom they work.

Reflections

1. Imagine yourself as the parent of a young child. What kind of information would you like to receive about your child and your child's classroom?

2. Think about a family you know particularly well. If this was the family of one of your students, how might you approach them to begin to develop a teacher–family relationship? Predict how they would react to different kinds of written communication, then follow up with a brief interview to confirm or question your predictions.

Field Experiences

1. Interview at least two early childhood educators. Ask them how often they send home letters, and how they think families react to this type of information.

2. Collect samples of teacher-to-family written communication. Compare and contrast the samples:
   - How much information about the classroom was shared?
   - Did the letters explain why certain activities were planned for the children?
   - Were there suggestions to families for how school learning could be extended at home?

3. Observe in a kindergarten class for at least two hours. Take notes about children's positive behaviors or accomplishments you could use as the basis for a note to send home to families. Try writing two or three of these brief notes.

Other Activities

1. Draft an introductory letter to families similar to the one in Box 6.1. Focus on the tone of your letter to ensure that you sound warm and open. Share your draft with at least two people, then revise the letter based on the feedback you receive.

2. Choose one age of young children. Work with a partner and write suggested activities for families and children to share. Be sure that the language you use is simple and yet informative.

3. Email is a very fast way of communication. Sometimes this speed and the informality of email can cause problems. If teachers are not careful with the language they use in emails, they may offend families without meaning to. Make a list of phrases that a teacher might write when writing quickly, and rewrite those to be more sensitive to families' feelings.

Further Reading

Diffily, D., & Morrison, K. (Eds.). (1997). *Family-friendly communication in early childhood programs.* Washington, DC: National Association for the Education of Young Children.

This book offers more than 90 brief articles explaining issues that relate to young children. The categories include Early Childhood Fundamentals, Around the Early Childhood Classroom, Learning Together at Home and School, Toward Literacy, Math and Science, Social-Emotional Development, and Family Matters. The book also suggests many other strategies for communicating with families.

Hollingsworth, H. L. (2001). We need to talk: Communication strategies for effective collaboration. *Teaching Exceptional Children, 33,* 6–9.

This article outlines a variety of communication strategies for communication with families, including conducting a needs assessment, producing newsletters, and forming study groups.

7

Shared Time with Families

Learning Objectives

The reader will learn and be able to discuss:

- Events that can be planned at the school level, such as Open House, Saturday School, and content area event nights

- Shared times that individual teachers can plan for the families of their students, including Meet-the-Teacher night, Family Meetings, conferences, and others

> The quality of the interpersonal relationship between family and program staff is typically viewed by the experts as the essential basis for strengthening child and family outcomes. The field now emphasizes relationship building as a core activity of the early childhood educator.
>
> —Douglas Powell, 2000

Relationships begin and are maintained in a variety of ways. One important practice that builds strong relationships is spending emotionally positive time together. It is easy to see that this principle is true for relationships among family members and friends. It is also true for relationships between teachers and family members.

Shared time between teachers and families provides opportunities for these people to get to know each other on a personal level. It also reinforces the sense that everyone is working toward a common goal that is best for the children. Shared time between teachers and families can occur at both the school level and the class level.

School Level

Schoolwide occasions such as Open House, Saturday School, or curriculum-related events such as Family Math Night, encourage families and teachers to spend time together. Everyone associated with the school is invited to attend these functions, and positive feelings about the school are promoted.

Open House

An open house typically occurs early in the academic year or during announced times that focus public attention on education, such as National Public School Week, Week of the Young Child, Dr. Seuss Birthday Celebration, or other such dates. Open house invitations are extended to family members—and sometimes, friends—of the students in the school.

When held in the first few weeks of the school year, this kind of celebratory event can set a positive tone for the whole year. Families who attend the open house have the opportunity to look around the school, see their children's classroom, glance at instructional materials, and meet teachers and staff. The actual time invested by parents to attend an open house is small. From the hour or so spent at an open house, parents feel more informed about their child's school. They get a feel for the place where their child spends his or her days, and at least have face and name recognition of adults with whom their child interacts on a daily basis.

Children also experience positive feelings about school during an open house. They have the opportunity to share their school with their parents and siblings. They give their parents a tour of the school and point out the things in their classrooms that are most meaningful to them. They explain their work that is posted around the classroom and talk about topics the class is studying. Family members almost always respond to their children in favorable, encouraging ways. The positive feedback children get from their parents at open house reinforces positive attitudes toward school.

Both students and their families tend to come away from this one event feeling better about school and each other. With such positive outcomes possible, teachers need to spend the time necessary for the event to be successful.

An open house will most likely be successful if:

- ☑ All students are involved in the preparation (children's encouragement is a strong influence on parents' attendance)
- ☑ The date is announced well in advance of the open house, and the event is well publicized
- ☑ The invitation lists the schedule for the evening (and explains that individual conferences cannot be held during the open house, but may be scheduled that night)
- ☑ There is an incentive for attending (e.g. a light meal such as sandwiches and chips or a give-away book for each family)
- ☑ Extra copies of school newsletters, handbooks, and forms are available for parents to take with them

Saturday School

Some elementary schools organize Saturday school. This event goes a step further than the unstructured gathering of an open house. Saturday school operates much like any other school day. The two exceptions are that parents, instead of students, attend, and the time is abbreviated. Classroom teachers follow their typical daily schedule and recreate recent learning experiences they have had with students. Specials teachers—P.E., art, music, computers—do the same. Parents even go through the lunch line in the cafeteria for a midmorning snack and have an outdoor recess time. Attending Saturday school helps families understand the types of experiences their children have at school. Parents understand the schedules their children keep and become familiar with all of the adults who are a part of their child's school life.

A Saturday school event will most likely be successful if:

- ☑ The event is organized to the point that every adult involved knows where they are supposed to be throughout the morning.
- ☑ The tone of the day is light.
- ☑ Each teacher plans a learning activity for families to experience rather than a lecture about their curriculum.
- ☑ The purpose for the day is as much about building relationships as it is about sharing information.

VOICES OF *Families*

Saturday school is the best school event I've ever attended. I learned more about my child's school and the way she spends her days during those three hours than from all the handbooks and newsletters I've ever read, and I read everything the school sends home. Just walking down the hall to PE when six other classes were in the halls was an experience in and of itself. I never thought about my daughter standing in line so she could wash her hands before lunch, or how long five minutes can feel if you are just sitting on the floor listening to announcements from the main office. Saturday school was a real learning experience for me. I know that the faculty and staff had to give up a weekend morning to do this, and I realize that something like this takes a lot of organization, but I think it was worth it. I really appreciate the time that teachers put into making our Saturday school happen.

Event Nights

Event nights are another way to share insights into the school curriculum with families. Instructional strategies that are currently used with young children are quite different from the way most adults remember learning. Curriculum-related event nights provide opportunities for adults to experience learning in ways that their child learns. Any content area of the school day can be the focus for an event night. Math tends to be a popular choice for many schools.

FAMILY MATH NIGHTS   A Family math night can help parents begin to understand how their children are learning math at school. A math night can be organized like a student math workshop. Lasting just over an hour, the whole group would meet together for a brief presentation about a math concept or an explanation about the school's approach to math instruction. Then, parents go to their child's classroom and choose among a menu of math activities that reinforce the large group presentation. Classroom teachers move around the room, interacting with adults in the same way they interact with students during the day. After working in small groups for 45 minutes or so, parents then return to the large group and share some of what they learned during their math work. This schedule helps parents begin to understand the school's approach to teaching mathematics, and experience the type of activities their children are involved in at school.

Any content area could be the focus of an evening devoted to helping families better understand the school's curriculum and common teaching strategies.

Beyond content areas, other parts of the school day could be featured by an event night.

FAMILY ART NIGHTS   A family art night can be an interactive time for parents and children to learn about and enjoy art together. A family art night can be arranged around notable artists and the different media they use. For example, one area in the school, perhaps a classroom, can have demonstrations about postimpressionist pointillism. The families can view Georges Seurat's work, then create their own painting in Seurat's style or fill in outline drawings by using markers to create dots of color. Other areas in the school could be set up similarly with other artists and their work.

Children's art work can be displayed in the halls, with children acting as docents. They would stand near the displays and inform adults about how the work was created, what media were used, and the style of the art.

It is a nice addition to the family art night to supply the families with a small packet of art supplies to take home. A reclosable bag can hold a fact sheet about an artist and simple supplies needed to create in that artist's style.

FAMILY PHYSICAL FITNESS NIGHTS   A family physical fitness night offers a nice balance of physical activity with information about health and wellness. Stations can be set up around the school for blood pressure testing, simple yoga exercises,

Family members and students play math games together at Family Math Night.

warm-up exercises, and nutrition information. Other stations might include presentations from community organizations such as the American Cancer Society about the effects of smoking, the local police department about driving under the influence of alcohol, or the local public health department about required vaccinations.

While these stations are available, the physical education teacher or other qualified adult can lead physical exercise sessions. By teaching parents and other important adults in the lives of children the exercises that the children do in PE classes, teachers are supporting life-long wellness for the entire family.

Not all event nights have to relate to learning experiences that children have at school. Sometimes, schools organize an event night that just focuses on a fun time to be shared by teachers and families. There are all kinds of activities that can be the basis for getting families together: bowling, softball, roller skating, miniature golf, or just sharing a meal. One school sponsored a family dance night where all the families met in the gymnasium on a Friday night. They did line dances and square dances for older children and adults. They danced the hokey pokey so the adults and all the children could dance together.

All of the events discussed in the preceding sections are organized for the entire school family. These help families better understand the school and its curriculum and build a sense of togetherness among the people who attend. However, many families feel uncomfortable in large groups of people in which they do not know other people. Some families need more of an incentive to arrange their schedules to spend an evening at their child's school. For these families, events arranged at the classroom level may encourage greater participation.

Classroom Level

As beneficial as schoolwide events are, shared time spent with the adults of just one class is different. Parents of students in one classroom have more in common with each other than parents of students in the entire school. Parents in one class have a child who spends large amounts of time with that one teacher and that particular group of children. Meetings among this smaller group of adults help them feel more comfortable as they get to know the other parents in the class. Also, the adults typically feel that this kind of meeting is more related to them personally.

Meet-the-Teacher Night

A meet-the-teacher gathering is typically held early in the school year so that families can spend some time in the classroom talking with their child's teacher. This is when teachers explain the logistics of the classroom. They talk about drop-off and pick-up routines and the school's lunch schedule. Teachers discuss recess, art, music, and computer times, and explain their approach to teaching reading, writing,

An agenda organizes information shared at meet-the-teacher night.

math, and other content areas. Teachers accept questions from parents, establishing the beginnings of ongoing conversations between teacher and families.

A meet-the-teacher night will most likely be successful if:

- ☑ Parents are informed about where to go when they arrive at school.
- ☑ Arrangements are made so that families who have more than one child in the school can attend the meetings in each child's class.
- ☑ The principal or director is visible and actively involved in the night.
- ☑ The event is at a convenient time for families.

Family Meetings

Some teachers continue having meetings for families throughout the year. Family meetings occur on a regular basis, usually once a month. The conversations between the classroom teacher and family members take several forms (Diffily, 2001). For a portion of the meeting, the teacher shares specific information about the classroom. She might open the meeting by explaining the reasons she encourages children to use developmental spelling or why she uses so many different math manipulatives. She shows student work and asks the adults to try out some learning

Family meetings offer a unique opportunity to learn about the life of a class.

Trandon is in the seventh grade now. Since he left first grade, he has had twelve different teachers and six different sets of classmates and their families. When I look at Trandon's closest friends, they are his classmates from first grade. When I think about the parents that I feel most comfortable talking with now, they are the parents from that first-grade class. Trandon's first-grade teacher made it a point to create a sense of community among her students, and she did the same sort of thing with the adults too. The family meetings during that first-grade year made the adults feel like we were working together for the benefit of all the students. We laughed in those meetings and we became sort of a family because of the meetings. Even now, six year later, I can still see results of all the things that our first-grade teacher did.

strategies on their own. As the adults try to encode sentences using developmental spelling, they come to understand how phonics is taught in the classrooms and how their children's writing will be more creative if they do not have to spell every word correctly. As the adults use linking cubes or two-colored counters to solve problems, they understand that math is more than computation and begin to appreciate that manipulatives help their children visualize problem-solving strategies.

As the adults work, the teacher inserts stories about how the children approach these same learning activities. The shared laughter about the stories and the conversation among the families support the relationships forming between the adults connected to this classroom.

Not all the talk is teacher-to-family. As the meeting continues, families take a more active role in the meetings. Some parents like to share anecdotes of what their child has done or said at home that gave them insight into the life of the class. Others like to share problematic moments they have had with their child and ask advice about parenting issues. At times, family members ask advice about such things as bedtime reading routines or how they can support their child's literacy or math development. At other times, parents like to get involved in planning activities for the class. The more the group meets together, the more the family meetings take on the characteristics of a group of friends getting together informally to talk about educational issues and their own children.

All of the people who attend family meetings have the opportunity to get to know one another better. Teachers and family members develop a stronger relationship, which facilitates other types of conversations between them. Conferences go more smoothly because they have already begun a partnership. Phone calls reporting a problem situation are accepted more readily because of the relationship between teacher and family that was created through family meetings. Relationships also develop among families. Simply getting to know other parents who have children of the same age and being able to talk about children this age is reassuring to many parents. Sharing learning activities, talking about the life of the classroom, and discussing children provides the beginning of relationships among families. These relationships among the adults establish an important foundation of educational support for the students, at school and at home (Swick, 1996).

VOICES *of Teachers*

I read about family meetings and all the good things that come from having these kinds of meetings. Intellectually, I can see the benefits. Emotionally, I was not sure that this was something I could do. Just thinking about having all these adults sitting around, looking at me, scared me. I kept thinking, "What if they ask a question I can't answer?" "What if I go blank and can't think of a thing to say?" "What if they gang up against me?" I could think of dozens of things that could go wrong. Then I would start rationalizing, "None of my teachers ever did this." "No one else in my building does these meetings." "My principal isn't even sure that this would be a good thing to do." "Why

put myself on the line when I am not even sure it will work?"

But I always returned to the stories I'd read about teachers who had class meetings, about how much closer the students were, how much more support these teachers had. I finally gave into my intellectual side and called my first family meeting. I only had five parents that first night. Now, it's a year later. I'm having more than twenty adults at each family meeting, and the results have been everything the articles promised—and more. Next year, I'll start having family meetings the first week of school. I'm convinced. The more time I spend with families, the more we all benefit—the children, the parents, and me.

A family meeting will most likely be successful if:

- ☑ The meeting is scheduled in advance.
- ☑ Notification is sent home more than once.
- ☑ Family members have input as to what night of the week the meeting is held and which hours best fit their schedules.
- ☑ The teacher makes the meeting a fun time for other adults—sharing entertaining stories about the children in class (obviously, after receiving permission from the parents of each child mentioned in the story).
- ☑ The teacher has sufficient time to share specific information about early childhood issues and learning occurring in the classroom.
- ☑ Families have time to ask questions, share stories about their children, and discuss parenting issues.

Usually a one- to two-hour block of time allows for the different types of "talk" that goes on during family meetings (Diffily, 2000).

Family–Teacher Conferences

Every family needs time to talk about their child individually and in private. Teachers provide this time through regularly scheduled conferences, as well as when the need arises to discuss a specific issue about a child. In these conferences, both the

Teachers share information about an individual child during a Family–Teacher conference.

teacher and the family members have time to talk. Teachers plan enough time for each conference so they can share representative samples of the child's work and discuss their observations of the child. They also plan approximately equal time to discuss questions, concerns, and ideas of the family.

Individual family conferences are excellent opportunities to share how one child works on a project. Using anecdotal records and documented observations or assessments, the teacher explains to the family what work their child did on a project and what the child learned by working on the different components. This is enhanced by sharing photographs of the child at work and explaining different work samples from the child's project folder. These conferences allow families to ask specific questions about class projects, and their child, and how he or she is doing in class.

A family/teacher conference will most likely be successful if the teacher:

☑ Creates a comfortable physical setting for the conference (adult-sized chairs, something to drink and/or eat)
☑ Is prepared to share work samples and discuss each child as a learner and as a member of the class
☑ Begins each conference by discussing positive information about the child
☑ Can suggest specific learning experiences families can provide to reinforce a child's strengths and support development in areas that need reinforcement

Family Visits to the Classroom

Confident teachers establish an open-door policy from the first day of school, allowing family members to spend time in the classroom as their schedule permits. Families can learn a great deal about their child and the way the classroom operates even during brief visits.

Adult visits to the classroom will most likely be successful if the teacher:

☑ Provides a couple of adult-sized chairs
☑ Displays children's work for family review
☑ Has a bulletin board with specific information for families
☑ Offers a small library of parenting books and magazines to lend to families
☑ Suggests specific times when families can experience certain types of learning activities, such as the class time for writing workshop; the class's computer lab time, when parents can join the children in experimenting with age-appropriate computer programs; the end of the day, when parents might be encouraged to join their children for a shared reading time

As families spend time in the class, they learn more about the work that children do and the routines the class follows. As family members spend more time in the class, many begin to feel comfortable enough with the teacher and the children to begin volunteering (Mapp, 1997).

Family Members Volunteering in the Classroom

Early childhood educators who see the benefits of having an open-door policy usually have more offers of assistance from the families of their students. Teachers can send home ideas for specific activities they need help with and that parents would feel comfortable doing. Box 7.1 is an example of a list that can be sent home at the first of the year.

Families volunteering in the classroom will most likely be successful if the teacher:

- ☑ Knows who is coming at what time of day
- ☑ Plans ahead of time what the volunteer will do
- ☑ Gives clear instructions to the volunteer

The teacher lets families know just how much she values having them in the classroom to work with the children and asks family members to consider volunteering. When families return the form and volunteer for a specific activity, the teacher follows through with those families very quickly. This lets them know that she was serious about their involvement in the class. Not all parents will be able to volunteer in the classroom, but the teacher should not assume that working parents cannot help. Many parents who work can arrange their schedules to go into work late one day a month or take an extra-long lunch hour if they feel that time spent in their child's class is important to the child and to the teacher.

Family members who volunteer in the classroom or at home to support the children's work feel they are a real part of the life of the class. Achieving this sense of belonging among families is worth several hours of the teacher's time spent facilitating volunteer opportunities.

BOX 7.1 | *Volunteer Opportunities*

- Read to a small group of children.
- Play math games with two or three children.
- Sponsor a 1-hour club on Friday mornings for 4-6 children.
- Assist with cooking experiences.
- Grocery shop for cooking experiences.
- Help set up art experiences.
- Drive for (or accompany the class on) field trips.
- Play musical instruments for the class.
- Check out books from the public library.
- Take dictation from individual children.
- Transcribe audio tapes.
- Matte children's paintings.
- Bind children's books.
- Supervise woodworking ventures.
  (Puckett and Diffily, 1999, p. 185)

Family members can volunteer to work with small groups of students

Special Events

Teachers also organize special event nights—or an end-of-the-school-day event—as a means to share information about young children and the classroom. Again, with three or four weeks' advance notice, most families can arrange their schedules so they can gather at school to help celebrate their children's accomplishments and to learn more about the way the class works. Poetry recitations, art evenings, math games, or child-published books can be the basis for inviting families to school.

These special events provide another opportunity for a teacher to talk with families. Before the event begins, the teacher spends a few minutes talking about what the children have done to prepare for the event and the learning that was embedded in the work. She also has the opportunity to talk with individual family members before and after the event.

A class-level event night will most likely be successful if:

☑ All students are involved in the preparation (children's encouragement is a strong influence on parents' attendance).

☑ The date is announced well in advance and the event is well publicized.

☑ The invitation tells what will occur that evening.

> **TIP**
>
> Consider helping children publish a book to be sent home after a special event. For example, after a poetry recitation event, help the children assemble the poems they have written or dictated. Photocopy the poems along with the accompanying illustrations and spiral bind them into a book for each family.

Family Field Trips

Another way teachers can share information about early childhood issues and learn more about families is through family field trips. Because some family members have difficulty taking time away from their jobs to spend time in the classroom, evening or weekend field trips allow most families to spend time with the teacher and with other families related to the class. If these field trips can be no-cost trips, then none of the families will be excluded because of financial reasons.

Field trips could be planned for anything that might interest families: a free play being produced by a local theater company, an art exhibit, a special storytime at the public library, or a field that has an abundance of spring wildflowers. Ideas for field trips are only as limited as the teacher's imagination.

As with other types of gatherings, families need as much advance notice as possible, and reminder notices like the one in Box 7.2 are sent home.

A family field trip will most likely be successful if:

- ☑ The date is announced well in advance and reminders are sent home.
- ☑ The field trip relates to something the class is studying so the parents feel they are extending their child's learning.
- ☑ The field trip is either no- or low-cost.

Home Visits

Home visits add another dimension to shared time between teachers and families. The shared times discussed in the preceding sections almost always occur at school. The school is a comfortable place for teachers, but as discussed in previous chapters, it is not necessarily comfortable for families.

BOX 7.2 | *Family Field Trip*

Saturday, April 23, 8:00 am to 10:00 am
Spring Wild Flowers

This note is for your refrigerator so you won't forget our next family field trip. There is a wonderful field within a mile of the school. It is filled with all kinds of spring wildflowers. We've read the book *Counting Wildflowers*, and used field guides to identify some wildflowers that I've brought into the class. I think you'll be impressed with how well your child can answer the questions that are asked in the field guides, leading to the identification of each flower. The children have become very skilled observers. I hope you and your family can join us for our wildflower trip. I think you'll have a good time, and might even learn some new facts about flowers. I will send home a map for how to get to the field in next week's folder.

Meeting together in a family's home may be uncomfortable for both parties. Teachers often worry about a variety of issues: not knowing what they might encounter, feeling awkward communicating with families in their homes, wondering how to deal with cultural and language differences, questioning conflicts in values, even doubting their personal safety in some neighborhoods (Boone and Barclay, 1995). Families also worry about allowing the teacher to come into their home. They wonder: What will the teacher think of our home? Will she think we are not good providers? Will she try to tell us how to raise our children? How long will she stay? (Boone and Barclay, 1995). With apprehensive feelings on both sides, it is often easier for teachers to decide not to do home visits. However, there is one overriding reason that teachers should consider before excluding home visits. "The most important aspect of a home visit . . . is the strong evidence that a teacher cares enough to move beyond the territorial confines of a classroom to reach out to a child and his family" (Gestwicki, 2000, p. 271).

Given that home visits can send such a strong positive message to families, it is invaluable for teachers to overcome some of their misgivings and invest some extra time to visit with families in their homes. A home visit will most likely be successful if:

- ☑ The parents set the day and time.
- ☑ The teacher makes the family feel comfortable within the first few minutes of the visit.
- ☑ The teacher interacts with the child so that the parents observe the relationship between teacher and child.

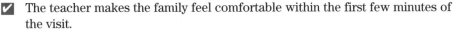

VOICES *of Families*

I have four kids older than Joshua, my first-grader. You can imagine my surprise when I got a note from Joshua's teacher saying she would like to come to our house and visit for about an hour. At first I couldn't believe that she just wanted to chat. I thought there had to be some big problem. Maybe Ms. Rodriquez had heard some bad stuff about our family, and was going to check it out. I didn't respond to the note. This morning, I talked to a friend of mine whose daughter is in Josh's class. She said Ms.

Rodriquez came to their house last week. She said Ms. Rodriquez brought some of Chelsea's work to show her, but that most of the time they just talked about things the class was doing and funny things Chelsea had said in class. Ms. Rodriquez sat down on the floor, held Chelsea in her lap, and read her a story. My friend was real impressed that Ms. Rodriquez made the time to come over. She said Ms. Rodriquez was real nice and really seemed to love Chelsea. I guess I'm going to invite her over to my house too.

This chapter shares many different ways an entire school or an individual class-room teacher can bring teachers and families together. It is critically important to note that neither a school nor an individual teacher should try to implement all of these events in a single academic year. Some schools and teachers do, in fact, sponsor all of these "shared times." Planning and implementing events like these takes time and effort. It is better to sponsor one or two successful events per year than to have several that are merely okay.

Informal Daily Conversations

Several formal ways that teacher and families can share time have been discussed in this chapter. However, it would be a mistake to overlook the importance of non-scheduled, informal daily conversations. For parents who drop off children in the mornings or pick them up in the afternoons, these opportunities for brief conversations can communicate quite a bit. The simple social courtesy of smiling and acknowledging family members lets them know that you appreciate them. Greeting parents at the door and welcoming them into the classroom for a few minutes would be better. A short conversation would be even better. Remembering to use their names and asking about other family members or some event in the family's life lets the family know that the teacher cares about them.

Conversations just before or after school need to be brief because a teacher's primary responsibility during those times is supervising children. Teachers need to communicate this to family members early in the school year so parents do not expect to have a long conversation or will not be offended if the teacher asks if they can set another time to talk. Another issue related to these before- or after-school conversations that teachers may have to address is the parent who does not stop to think about the inappropriateness of some discussions. Adults should not discuss one child or any other confidential issue where children or other adults can overhear the conversation.

Even though teachers may have to help shape appropriate conversations during the before- and after-school times, strong relationships can be initiated and fostered through these brief conversations. Teachers can share short stories about an individual child's accomplishment that day, something a child said that showed particular insight, or just a comical moment. Family members appreciate hearing these stories and knowing that a teacher observes their child closely enough to be aware of these incidents.

Obviously these conversations cannot occur if children ride a bus to school or are part of a car pool. Teachers have to use other methods of communicating with family members who do not come to the school.

Summary

Relationships between teachers and family members are strengthened by spending shared time together. Shared times can be planned for the entire school or for those families associated with one class. Schoolwide events offer family members opportunities to learn more about the school, its schedule, the curriculum, and teaching strategies frequently used by teachers. Class-level events offer many of the same opportunities, while being more intimate and supporting closer relationships between one teacher and the adults associated with the students in a single class.

Reflections

1. Early childhood educators feel comfortable working with young children; however, many teachers begin feeling uncomfortable when they even think about spending a few hours with the adults in the lives of their students. Working in small groups, generate a list of specific issues that might make teachers feel uncomfortable working with family members.
2. In these same groups, generate a second list of things a teacher might do to make herself feel more comfortable in large group settings, such as family meetings or family field trips.

 ## Field Experiences

1. Identify an early childhood educator who holds regular family meetings. Ask if you can attend one of the meetings. Observe the interactions between the teacher and the family members and take notes to discuss in class.
2. Contact a local elementary school and ask permission to attend their next schoolwide event night (open house, family math night, family arts night, a school carnival, a school festival, etc.). Observe the interactions between the teacher and the family members and take notes to discuss in class.
3. Search your local community for possible no-cost/low-cost places that would be appropriate for family field trips.

Other Activities

1. Plan an event night (on paper). What would the differences be in planning for one class versus planning for an entire school?
2. In small groups, make a list of "things to consider" in planning and making home visits to students' homes.

 ## Further Readings

Cesarone, B. (2000). Parent-teacher conference. *Childhood Education, 76,* 180–181.

    Cesarone summarizes journal articles and ERIC documents related to planning and implementing successful parent–teacher conferences.

Clark, A. *Parent-teacher conferences: Suggestions for parents.* ERIC Document Reproduction Service 433965

    Parent–teacher conferences can often be filled with anxiety on both parts. This Digest article is to be shared with families so that they can be better prepared for a conference about their child.

Cline, Z. (2001). Reading parties: Helping families share the joy of literacy. *The Reading Teacher, 55,* 236–237.

    This article shares the implementation of a unique program that combines home visits with family reading nights. The families take turns hosting reading parties in their homes as an opportunity to learn about how to create a literate environment in their homes and support their children's literacy development.

Diffily, D. (2001). Family meetings: Building relationships between the teacher and families. *Dimensions of Early Childhood, 29,* 5–10.

    This article describes monthly meetings between the classroom teacher and the families of the students in that class. It covers timing, planning, topics of discussion, and benefits of such meetings.

Quiroz, B., Greenfield, P. M., & Altchech, M. (1999). Bridging cultures with a parent-teacher conference. *Educational Leadership 56,* 68–70.

    This article shares the story of one teacher who tried student-led conferences. These were not well received by recent Hispanic immigrant families.

Taking the families' concerns into consideration, the teacher revised the conferences to be a group conference format.

Rose, M. C. (1998). Handle with care: The difficult parent–teacher conference. *Instructor 108*, 92–93, 101.

This article offers suggestions to teachers facing a difficult conference with parents. Before the conference, teachers should make sure that the difficulties are documented, communicate concerns to the parents in writing, and ask for their support. At the conference, they should welcome parents, take notes, choose their words carefully, seek parents' suggestions, and consider asking the principal to the meeting. After the conference, they should follow up and keep communicating.

Southworth, S. A. (2000). Talk time: Communicate effectively with parents, and maximize students' school success. *Instructor, 110*, 31–32.

This article presents suggestions about how teachers can build positive, strong relationships with parents or caregivers, including: telephone parents before an open house or in-person meeting; start the first conference by asking parents to share what is happening at home; be aware of different cultures, values, and parenting styles; and enlist parent input.

Strudler, R. (1993). Doesn't he have beautiful blue eyes? Tips for a successful parent–teacher conference. *Preventing School Failure, 37*, 11–13.

Strudler gives tips for successful parent–teacher conferences concerning children with special needs, such as reducing stress levels and involving parents positively.

Szemcsak, D. D., & West, O. J. (1996). The whole town is talking about it . . . "Math month. That is." *Teaching Children Mathematics, 3*, 179–173.

This article describes a school's effort to involve parents, students, and teachers in updating their math instruction. The programs include a family math night, a newsletter devoted specifically to mathematics, and math speakers at special mathematics events.

8

FAMILY TEACHERS COMMUNITY

Other Ways to Communicate

Learning Objectives

The reader will learn and be able to discuss the benefits of and how to create:

- Parent bulletin boards
- Parent resource rooms
- Parent resource libraries
- Curriculum materials lending libraries
- Interactive homework
- Effective phone calls with family members
- Websites

> There are no set formulas for creating
> effective family partnership programs.
> Instead, educators must ask questions about the particular
> situation and build family–school collaboration on
> the answers they receive.
>
> —International Reading Association, 2002

Written information, as discussed in Chapter 6, and shared time with families, as discussed in Chapter 7, are important ways to establish relationships between teachers and families and to support family involvement. However, there are other ways of communicating with families that should not be ignored. At the school level, educators could consider creating parent bulletin boards, parent resource rooms, parent lending libraries, and lending libraries for curriculum materials. On a smaller scale, classroom teachers could put these ideas into practice. Teachers can also use telephones, email, and websites to communicate with families.

School Level

Parent Bulletin Boards

A simple way of communicating with families that does not require many resources is a bulletin board in the school that is dedicated to information for families. Creating a space explicitly to communicate with families sends the message that families are respected in this school. A bulletin board for this purpose should be near an area where families drop off or pick up their children. It should look appealing and be updated on a regular basis to keep attracting family members.

VOICES *of Families*

I am forever losing important papers that the center sends home. It is embarrassing to have to ask the teacher for another copy of something. I think I had to ask for extra sets of emergency cards three times before I actually filled them out and returned them to the school. I love the fact that the center director has started a parent bulletin board. If I lose something, all I have to do is drop by the bulletin board to get a second copy of whatever it was that I lost. She also chooses some really good articles about parenting and helping to support your child's learning. Every week she puts out two or three articles, and I pick up the new articles every Monday afternoon. That way I have something with me to read when I find myself waiting in line at the bank or the grocery store, or while I'm waiting for soccer practice to be over. I really like the new parent bulletin board.

A parent bulletin board offers all kinds of written information for families.

This bulletin board could hold copies of school notes or newsletters that were sent home in the past two or three weeks. This would help noncustodial parents stay informed and provide copies for parents who have lost the papers that were sent home. It could also have announcements of upcoming school events that would interest parents, advertisements of parent meetings or special event nights, copies of informational brochures or articles that might interest families, school lunch menus, and reminders about deadlines for such things as book order forms or permission slips for field trips.

The parent bulletin board could also feature one class in the school in a way that shares information with families about children's learning. Photographs of learning centers with an explanation of the learning that takes place in each center shares important information with families about how the environment supports children's learning. Photographs of the students at work in a classroom posted alongside work samples and a written explanation from the teacher (or the students themselves) about the learning that took place communicates how children learn a particular concept or skill. These bulletin boards can and should be displayed outside of classrooms, but few families wander throughout the school looking at all the bulletin boards. Having rotating displays on or near the school's parent bulletin board communicates positively about children's learning to all family members—and all visitors to the school.

Parent Resource Room

Although it is not always possible, dedicating an entire room to families sends a strong message about how much the school values families. When an extra room is available within a school, having it set aside for parents serves many purposes. It can house resources for families, such as magazines and books, and with the addition of a coffee pot and a few comfortable chairs, this room could become a place for family members to spend a few quiet minutes after they drop off children in the mornings or before they pick up children in the afternoons.

This room can be an informal meeting place for family members that facilitates interaction with other parents. It could be used for parents and teachers to have a private place for conferences. Parenting skills classes, parents as teachers classes, or other activities involving parents could be held in the parent resource room. Parents who are not comfortable in classrooms may feel comfortable in a neutral room such as the parent resource room.

Parent Lending Library

A parent lending library provides valuable learning experiences for family members. This library can be relatively small and can be housed in either the parent resource room or in the school's library. Parents who might not take the time to go to a bookstore or a public library might check out a parenting book if it is easily available to them.

Curriculum materials that can be checked out extend a child's learning at home.

BOX 8.1 | *Suggested Adult Books for a Parents' Lending Library*

Calkins, L. M., & Bellino, L. (1998). *Raising lifelong learners: A parents' guide.* Cambridge, MA: Perseus Press.

Cullinan, B. E. (2000). *Read to me: Raising kids who love to read.* New York: Scholastic.

Dyer, W. W. (2001). *What do you really want for your children?* New York: Avon Books.

Galinsky, E., & David, J. (1991). *The preschool years: Family strategies that work—From experts and parents.* New York: Ballantine.

Glenn, H. S., & Nelsen, J. (2000). *Raising self-reliant children in a self-indulgent world,* 2nd ed. Rocklin, CA: Prima Publishing.

Nelsen, J., Duffy, R., & Erwin, C. (1998). *Positive discipline for preschoolers: For their early years—Raising children who are responsible, respectful, and resourceful.* Rocklin, CA: Prima Publishing.

Rich, D. (1998). *Megaskills: Building children's achievement for the information age.* New York: Mariner Books.

Stipek, D., & Seal, K. (2001). *Motivated minds: Raising children to love learning.* Berkeley, CA: Owl Press.

Trelease, J. (2001). *The read-aloud handbook,* 5th ed. New York: Penguin.

Curriculum Materials Lending Library

Just as books can be checked out, learning materials also can be checked out for parents to use when working with their children. Again, these materials can be housed in either the parent resource room or in the school's library. These materials could include book bags with books and suggestions of ways to extend the book, or math manipulatives with instructions for games at various grade levels. Science kits could be created with all the materials needed for a particular experiment.

Many families are willing to work with their children on school-related activities, but simply do not know what to do. When the school provides the materials and specific instructions on how to work with a child in a particular grade—and makes these materials easily accessible—parents are more likely to check out materials and use them with their children. A curriculum resource library requires a substantial initial investment and ongoing funding to replace materials. This would require a strong commitment on the part of the budget committee of a school.

These are a few ways of communicating with families beyond written communication and shared time. On a smaller scale, classroom teachers could implement these ideas of a parent bulletin board, a parent resource room (which in a single classroom would have to be a corner), a parent lending library, or a curriculum resource library.

VOICES *of Children*

The day of the weekend, me and my mom go to the kids' library and pick out a game for the weekend. There are special games there that you can't even buy at the store. Me and my mom pick out one to take home and we play it on Friday night and Saturday night and Sunday night. That's three nights.

VOICES of Administrators

When my teachers first came to me with the idea of having a library of materials that families could check out, my first reaction was, "This could cost a lot of money." My second thought was, "How well will families take care of these materials?" My third thought was, "How much time is it going to take to keep up with what gets lost, and how much money will I have to allocate to keep materials up to date?" All I could think about was the negative aspects. I talked with directors of other centers and their reactions were split half and half. Half of them thought much like I did, at first. The other half talked to me about how much their families used the curriculum resources library they had.

After a lot of thought, I decided to go with the idea. We scheduled a "make-it-take-it"

night for families. We all made games that were appropriate for young children. Parents who were there took a few of the games home, but left one or two for the center. All the teachers left theirs for the center. So that one night, we had about fifteen games to put in the resources library. Over the next six months, I invested about $100 each month to purchase items for the library, and we had another "make-it-take-it" night. Within a year, we had a nice collection of books and games that families could check out, and they used them fairly often. And, they took care of the things.

My initial reactions were all negative, but I admit, I was wrong. This was a very good thing to do for the families of our students.

Classroom Level

There are additional ways that classroom teachers can communicate with families. Teachers can create interactive homework and use the telephone, email, and websites to share information with parents.

Interactive Homework

Interactive homework has been suggested as a superior strategy for encouraging family involvement with a child's education (Epstein, 2001). When the teacher assigns homework that is to be completed by children and parents working together, it gives parents a meaningful reason to interact with their child about school learning. The general parent/child conversation about "what happened in school" turns into a more specific conversation about a particular area of learning. In an interview, Joyce Epstein (Jones, 2001) said, "Interactive homework should be a regular, but not nightly, activity. Once a week, or once every other week, is fine. Every night should not be interactive homework. It really is a matter of having a family-friendly schedule."

Phone Calls

Teachers often use the telephone to communicate with families. All too often phone calls from a teacher are about some kind of a problem—a child who has become sick during the day or a report about inappropriate behavior in class. The telephone can, and should be, used more often to report good news. During the day, teachers can use part of the lunch time or other breaks to call a parent and briefly describe an event in which their child tried something new, said something humorous, or was particularly kind to another child. Evening phone calls made to families who do not read English can share information from the weekly letters or tell parents about objects children have been asked to bring to school.

Another way to use telephones is using a speaker phone. Typically phone calls are between one teacher and one parent. Using a speaker phone at school allows several teachers to participate in a conference with a parent. The child can even be included in this type of telephone conference. Add three-way calling and more than one parent can be part of the conference. Miscommunication happens less often when all interested parties are involved in one conference rather than each teacher talking with the family separately (Chaboudy, Jameson, and Huber, 2001).

Not all phone calls have to actually talk with a family member. Sometimes leaving a message on the answering machine is just as effective—and it takes even less time than talking with a parent. Messages can be left for working parents on their home answering machine. Parents welcome a positive message from their child's teacher after a long day at work.

Parents always welcome a phone call to let them know that their son has announced to the class, "My dad knows everything about building stuff. He can build us a museum," or that their daughter has proclaimed, "My mom knows everything about dinosaurs. We have lots and lots of dinosaur bones in our yard. I'll dig some up and bring them tomorrow." Telephone calls do not need to be long and they can be used in a variety of ways to share information with families.

Websites

Even though not all families have a computer with Internet access in their homes, many families can access a computer or the Internet through their jobs or in public libraries. When class information is on a

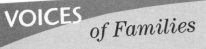

VOICES *of Families*

This teacher was different. Before her, the only time I heard from a teacher was when my son was in trouble. The first time I heard her voice on my answering machine, it was the second week of school, I thought, "here we go again." But this wasn't a message about something Demetrian had done wrong. It was a message telling me about how he had helped a child on the playground who fell down. That message made me feel so good. And, that wasn't the only "good" message I got that year. That teacher called every month or so with a little story about Demetrian and something good he had done. That doesn't mean that she never called to talk about something Demetrian had done that was wrong, but it was easier for me to take when I knew that she was going to call with bad news *and* she was going to call with good news.

website, families can access information twenty-four hours a day. Extended family members also can access this information, no matter where they are in the world. Teachers can create a website that is relatively simple and not very time-consuming.

Some teachers are using the Blackboard program to create rather detailed websites. This program has a series of templates that are very user-friendly. Following is a list of various sections of the Blackboard program and information typically posted in those sections:

- ☑ *Home Page:* basic announcements about topics the class is studying, projects, conferences, field trips, and special events. Information on this page can be programmed to erase itself every two weeks and send that information to an archives section.
- ☑ *Course Info Section:* learning objectives for particular assignments, grading scales, and class rules
- ☑ *Staff Info:* email addresses, home phone numbers, classroom extensions, and photographs of the classroom teacher and other faculty and staff who interact with students in this class
- ☑ *Course Documents:* forms such as reading logs, observation logs, and photographs of the class at work
- ☑ *Assignments:* requirements for long-term assignments along with connected learning objectives, project requirements, and deadlines
- ☑ *Communications:* a secure chat room, student web pages, and a bulletin board
- ☑ *External Links:* timely websites that support classroom learning
- ☑ *Student Tools:* student-created web pages, student grades, personal calendars, and the ability to send computer-generated projects to the teachers

There is a learning curve when teachers begin creating websites. At first, this task may seem time-consuming, but within a few weeks adding to or updating parts of a website does not consume much time at all.

Real-Time Video

Real-time video of classrooms, available to parents through the Internet with a special password, allows family members to observe their child's class in progress. At this time, this is rare—limited to a few upscale child care centers and elementary schools. But it is possible that it will become more widespread as the technology costs decrease and family demand increases.

VOICES *of Children*

My teacher put our whole class on a website. I wrote down the address on a special card and I keep it with me all the time. I went to my grandmother's house and typed the address on her computer. Grandma could see my room and all my friends and my teacher and some of the work I did. I went to my uncle's house and I typed the address on his computer. He got to see all that same stuff that Grandma got to see. I can go anywhere they have a computer and show them my class.

VOICES of Families

Going back to work after my six-month maternity leave was absolutely horrible. I wanted to stay home with my baby, but it was simply not something I could do. Luckily, I work for a forward-thinking company. We have on-site corporate child care. My baby is just downstairs. I can drop in whenever I have time to spend with my child. And, when I can't get away from my office, I can log on to the passworded website and watch the infant room. The camera is set up in a way that I can see almost everything that goes on in the room. I can see her playing on the floor or taking a bottle from one of the infant caregivers. I know that this is not available for all mothers. I wish it was. It makes all the difference in me being able to work and be in a relatively good mood and being miserable all the time wondering what my daughter is doing. I will be loyal to this company forever for making my job as a mother and my job as an employee doable.

Summary

Just as classroom teachers teach the same concept in many ways to reach all learners, teachers need to use multiple ways to share information with families. Families who do not respond to written communication or attend meetings may respond to telephone calls or emails. They may also use resources such as websites, parent bulletin boards, parent resource rooms, parent lending libraries, and curriculum materials lending libraries.

Reflections

1. Consider all the ways of communicating with families mentioned in this chapter. Make a list of all the methods from most expensive to least expensive. Make a separate list of all the methods from most time-consuming to least time-consuming. Based on these two factors, choose one or two methods that would be easiest for you to implement.

2. Consider each method of communicating with families mentioned in this chapter from the perspective of a family member. Which method(s) do you think would best meet the needs of families at an elementary school you have visited? Formulate a rationale for the method(s) you selected.

Field Experiences

1. Visit two or three elementary schools. Walk through all the halls of the school, looking for physical evidence of the school's attempts to communicate with families.

2. Interview two to three families and ask if their child's teacher uses technology in any way to communicate with them and, if so, how?

3. Think about a website you'd like to create for your first class. List the components you think are important and begin to construct a sample website.

Other Activities

1. Working in small groups, design and hang a parent bulletin board for parents of prekindergarten children and one for parents of third-grade students. Discuss how the difference in the children's ages changes the information posted on the bulletin

board and the resources that were most helpful in age-appropriate information.

2. Discuss the aesthetics of the bulletin boards and determine how the format might be changed to be more appealing. Consider ways to involve the children in the construction of the bulletin board as well as colors and designs.

Further Readings

Chaboudy, R., Jameson, P., & Huber, J. (2001). Connecting families and schools through technology. *Book Report, 20,* 52–58.

This article describes ways that technology can enhance communication between teachers and families, such as email, speaker phones, electronic portfolios/conferences, and websites.

Clark, A. (1999). *Parent-teacher conferences: Suggestions for parents.* ERIC Reproduction Service Number 433965

This ERIC Digest was written to share with families. It shares ways that parents can help to improve parent–teacher conferences. Suggestions include asking what is being done to help a child overcome a problem, asking about the teacher's expectations, creating a plan together with the teacher, and scheduling a follow-up conference. The Digest points out that even if a child is not experiencing difficulties, parents can contribute to the effectiveness of the conference by asking questions such as, "What can I do at home to support what is being done at school?"

Faucette, E. (2001). Are you missing the most important ingredient? A recipe for increasing student achievement. *MultiMedia Schools, 7,* 56–58, 60–61.

Focusing on increasing parent involvement, this article discusses how library and media specialists can assist with getting families more involved in schools.

Jongsma, K. (2001). Literacy links between home and school. *The Reading Teacher, 55,* 58–61.

Jongsma describes literacy backpacks and writing suitcases that go back and forth from school to home to encourage families to work with their children using the materials and activities included in both.

Love, F. E. (1996). Communicating with parents: What beginning teachers can do. *College Student Journal, 30,* 440–444.

This article offers a variety of techniques designed to assist beginning and experienced teachers toward positive communication with parents. Includes writing introductory letters and parents' bulletin boards.

Nistler, R. J., & Maiers, A. (1999). Exploring home-school connections: A family literacy perspective on improving urban schools, *Education and Urban Society, 32,* 3–17.

Focusing on Hispanic families, the authors discuss effective teaching practices that connect home and school and conversations between teachers and Latino parents during parent/teacher conferences.

Websites to Explore

- Houston Public Library and The Children's Museum of Houston
  http://www.hpl.lib.tx.us/youth/prl_links.html
  These two community resources joined together to create a virtual parents resource library, focused on children's literature.
- Reading Matters
  http://www.readingmatters.net/
  Click on "parent involvement" and you will go to the page that focuses on families working with their children (related to reading). Suggestions for books for a lending library are suggested under the link "parent resource library."

9

FAMILY
TEACHERS
COMMUNITY

Working through Cultural Differences between Teacher and Families

Learning Objectives

The reader will learn and be able to discuss characteristics of:

- African American families
- Hispanic families
- Asian families
- Native American families
- Middle Eastern families
- immigrant families
- potential differences among different cultural groups

> A person's cultural identity exerts a profound influence
> on his or her lifeways, but it is not the only critical factor.
> Every individual and every family is defined
> by more than these characteristics.
>
> —Eleanor Lynch and Marci Hanson, 1997

It does not matter how large or small a group is or what its primary function is. Whenever a group of people spend any amount of time together, there will be differences among people. There will most likely be conflicts.

No matter how nice a teacher is or how much she reaches out to families, there will inevitably be times when she misunderstands a parent or a parent misunderstands her. A primary area of difference is often related to culture. When teachers are aware of some of the differences that might exist between them and parents, they are better prepared to work through the differences and may be able to avoid conflicts. Some cultural differences are discussed in this chapter.

Most early childhood educators are middle-class white women. Many have not had extensive experience with other cultures. This chapter presents information about African American families, Hispanic families, Asian families, Native American families, Middle Eastern families, and immigrant families. Although there is as much difference within a cultural group as there is between that cultural group and the middle-class white culture, there are some similarities within a culture. Rather than discuss the characteristics of families from different cultures from an objective, academic perspective, the characteristics of families are presented by one early childhood educator who is part of that culture. Following the discussion about the characteristics of families from each cultural group, a case study written by a middle-class, white, early childhood educator is presented, along with a response from the early childhood educator from that cultural group.

Each early childhood educator in this chapter is sensitive about her culture and does not want to stereotype an entire culture. However, they want to share some of the characteristics of their culture and, in doing so, help preservice teachers understand other cultures a bit better.

As strong an influence as culture and its characteristics is on a family, there are other factors that also shape the ways that individuals and families live. These mitigating factors include the following:

☑ Socioeconomic status
☑ Educational level
☑ Time of arrival in the United States
☑ Premigration and migration experiences
☑ Proximity to other members of their cultural or ethnic community
☑ Proximity to other cultural groups
☑ Age
☑ Gender
☑ Language proficiency
☑ Sociopolitical climate, including the extent of societal bias, distrust, and racism (Lynch and Hanson, 1997, p. 496)

Cultural Differences

Sometimes cultural beliefs and traditions are very easily identified. People's actions and interactions are influenced by the culture in which they were raised. While these influences are present, people are often unaware of them. The differences in the culture of a teacher and a family can cause difficulty. To avoid some of these conflicts, teachers can spend time reflecting on their own culture and values and investigating other cultures/values. In the following sections, five cultures are discussed—African American, Hispanic, Asian, Native American, and Middle Eastern—as is the culture of immigrant families.

Characteristics of African American Families

Lynch and Hanson (1997) list seven differences between African American beliefs, values, and practices and those of the mainstream culture.

BOX 9.1 | *Contrasting Beliefs, Values, and Practices*

African American Culture	Mainstream Culture
Collective orientation	Individual orientation
Kinship and extended family bonds	Nuclear and immediate family bonds
High-context communication	Low-context communication
Religious, spiritual orientation	More secular orientation
More authoritarian child-rearing practices	More permissive child-rearing practices
Greater respect for elderly and their role in the family	Less respect for the role of elderly in the family
More oriented to situation than to time	More oriented to time than to situation

From Lynch and Hanson, 1997, p. 203

One African American Early Childhood Educator and How She Describes African American Families

HELEN PERKINS is an African American wife, mother, and teacher. She taught elementary school for nineteen years and supported other teachers for three years as a lead reading teacher in the Dallas Independent School District. She currently teaches preservice teachers in the Center for Teacher Education at Southern Methodist University in Dallas, Texas.

"There are two types of typical African American families. One is an average suburban family: a mother, father, and two or three children. The other is the average inner-city family, which is typically a mother and grandmother raising four or five children.

"Roles in these two family types are different. In the suburban family it is common for both parents to work, with the mother also assuming most of the responsibilities for the children. She takes care of the children's physical and emotional needs. In the urban family the mother and the grandmother share caretaking responsibilities for the children. It is not unusual for the grandmother to take on more of these responsibilities because the mother may work more than one job. She is not physically in the home to take care of her children, so the grandmother takes over many of these responsibilities.

"No matter the composition of the nuclear family, African Americans value family very highly, and the extended family is just as important as the nuclear family. In fact, the sense of family extends beyond the extended family. People who show a high level of love and affection for a family's children are deemed family. Close friends are often treated—and even referred to—as family members. It is not unusual for children to call their parents' close friends 'aunt' or 'uncle.' Friends who have this type of relationship with a family usually have close bonds with the children and are just as likely as the parents to offer advice to or discipline the children.

"When it comes to interacting with schools, in the suburban families it is the mother who gets children ready for school, takes them to school, reminds them about their homework, and attends all parent–teacher conferences. Fathers typically go to the school only when a child has a problem or is involved in a sporting event or activities such as PTA performance and band or choir performances. In urban families, few mothers, fathers, or grandparents are involved with their children's schools.

"Education is valued very highly in most African American homes. Parents want their children to become successful adults, and they view education as the way to reach this success. However, many African American families do not know how to support children's education. The vast majority of African American parents trust the school to educate their children. When they trust the teacher, they view her or him as an authority figure in their children's lives. They teach their children to respect the teacher and be obedient. However, this trust is not automatic. African American parents tend to hold back and observe teachers. They look for signs that teachers love their children. When they see this, teachers are truly trusted. If they do not perceive that to be the case, they tend to stay away from the school and avoid the teacher."

Case Study

This is my third year to teach kindergarten, but my first in this school. The school is predominately African American. I am white. I am having problems getting parents to come to the school, and I am beginning to think that it may be because I am white. Parents come and talk to the other teachers around me. They come to conferences. They even hang out in some of the classrooms and just chat with those teachers at the end of the day.

I don't understand it. I send letters to all the families of my students every week. I've been told that a lot of families at this school don't know how to help their children, so every Friday I write about what I've been doing with their children during the week and what they should be doing at home so their children will learn more.

I put out a sign-up sheet for end-of-the-first-six-weeks' parent–teacher conferences. The conferences were 15 minutes long, scheduled every 20 minutes. That way I could get three conferences done in an hour. I was organized and prepared. I had individual folders for each student. I had detailed plans for what each family needed to do to help their child and told them that in my weekly letter home. Very few parents signed up. Even fewer families actually showed up.

I feel that I am doing more than my part in working with families. I am trying to help them help their children. If they were really interested in helping their children be successful in school, they would read my letters and do those home activities. They would come up to school and talk to me every so often. At the very least, they would come to a parent–teacher conference so that I could tell them what they need to be doing with their child. I don't know what more I can do to get these families to care about their children's education.

Response from the African American Early Childhood Educator: Helen's Response to the Case Study

It is fairly obvious that this teacher expects parents to show their love and support for their children in ways that she has determined to be the "right" ways. Because the parents are not coming to the school and talking to her, she has decided that the parents do not care about their children's education.

She doesn't realize that the African American families are most likely staying away from the school because of her. She probably does not realize that she started building a wall between herself and the families of her students with the very first letter she sent home. In that first letter, she began telling parents what they needed to be doing with their children. She did not take the time to begin developing relationships with the families. She just jumped in and started telling them what they needed to do. When she tried to set up parent–teacher conferences, again she set herself up as the expert on children who was going to tell parents what they needed to be doing with their children. African American families are going to see this behavior as condescending.

African American families want to know that a teacher cares for their child before they will accept the teacher's advice as being best for their child. The teacher would have had more success with the families of her students if she had worked on relationships first. She should get to know as much as she can about each child's background. When she talks to the parents, she should respect them as adults, not talking down to them. She also needs to be careful with tone and facial expression. African Americans read body language as much as they listen to the words being spoken.

The teacher could have set up a better situation with parents if she had called the parents before the school year began to welcome them to her class, or even in the first week of school to say something nice about their child. Phone calls like this can help establish a relationship between the teacher and parents. These calls show that a teacher cares. Another thing this teacher might consider would be to do some things in the community of the school: attending a sports game or community event, shopping in local stores. This is an extension of showing that the teacher cares. This begins to establish trust, and African American parents are more receptive to any suggestions once they trust the teacher.

The parents who did not come to the conferences were not showing that they did not care about their children. They were showing that they did not trust the teacher. They were choosing not to interact with the teacher.

Characteristics of Hispanic Families

Just as in African American families, there is probably as much difference among Hispanic families as between Hispanic families and Caucasian families. However, it is helpful to be aware of general differences between what Lynch and Hanson refer to as the Latino culture and the mainstream culture (1997). Some of the differences in values are listed in Box 9.2.

One Hispanic Early Childhood Educator and How She Describes Hispanic Families

LINDA RAMOS is a Hispanic teacher, wife, and mother. She has a master's degree in elementary education from Texas Christian University. She is certified to teach prekindergarten through eighth grade and is endorsed in English as a second language, bilingual, gifted, and early childhood education. Linda has spent thirty-one years working in the Fort Worth Independent School District, twenty-five years in the classroom, and six years working on an instructional support team. From the beginning of her career, she had two primary goals: first, to help Hispanic children set higher goals for themselves and feel that they were capable of achieving academically, and second, to help other adults have similarly high expectations for Hispanic students.

BOX 9.2 *Contrasting Beliefs, Values, and Practices*

Hispanic Cultures	Mainstream Culture
Collective orientation	Individual orientation
Interdependence	Independence
Collective, group identity	Individual identity
Cooperation	Competition
Relaxed with time	Time sensitivity
Emphasis on interpersonal relations	Emphasis on task orientation
Tendency toward patriarchal family structure	Tendency toward democratic family structure
Relaxed about child development	Strong expectations for child development
Extended family system more pronounced	Nuclear family system more pronounced

Adapted from Lynch and Hanson, 1997

"Among Hispanics, there is a strong sense of family. Hispanic families are very close in many ways. If there is a special celebration like a wedding, or a special problem like a funeral or an illness in the family, the whole family comes together. And it is not just the immediate family. All kinds of aunts, uncles, and cousins show up for these events. Food is almost always part of these events. Food is important in the Hispanic culture. Eating brings people together—not just for celebrations, but in every day ways too. Everyone knows that they can drop in at a family's or friend's house, and there will be food in the refrigerator. You may have just finished a meal at home, but if you drop in to visit grandmother, you'll find yourself eating again within a few minutes of walking through the front door. That tradition may be dying away a bit with fast food becoming so dominant in today's society, but it is still evident in many Hispanic families.

"Even though families are close to each other in most Hispanic cultures, that does not mean that the members of the immediate family are close. There is a distance between most fathers and their children. The love is there, but there is not a physical closeness, and fathers are just not part of the caretaking of children. There is some difference between daughters and sons. For fathers, there is a strong sense of pride related to having a son. Still, the father does not do much in terms of taking care of young sons. In a lot of Anglo families, you see a special relationship between fathers and daughters—"daddy's little girls." You don't see that very much in Hispanic families. The fathers don't do much with young boys. They do even less with young girls. The mother is the one who takes care of the children. She is the one who brings the family together.

"There is a difference in how boys and girls are treated from an early age. Boys usually have the freedom to go outside and play in or around the neighborhood, but girls are expected to stay home. Mothers are more protective of girls. Girls are expected to learn how to care for the house and care for siblings from an early age. There are not these same expectations for boys.

"This sense that the woman is responsible for the family is pervasive among Hispanic families. It sounds old-fashioned, but women are seen as those who serve others. This attitude is passed down from generation to generation. It keeps many young Hispanic females from even thinking about going to college or being leaders in the community or in the workplace. Add this attitude of service together with lack of male affection from fathers and the fact that most Hispanic families do not talk about intimate issues such as sex, and you have a lot of teenage pregnancies in Hispanic families.

"Hispanics view education as the responsibility of teachers. They generally do not feel they have the right to question educators. They feel that going into a class during the day is interrupting the class, something they should not do.

"Thinking back to my own parents, they were not involved in my education. As a child in elementary school, I wanted my mother to be a homeroom mother. She didn't work. She could have done that, but she didn't feel she should be doing that kind of thing. When I came home, we didn't talk about school. I don't remember my parents ever helping with homework or even asking me if I had homework. I saw that in a lot of Hispanic families when I was young. I see that same thing today. Most Hispanics see home and school as very separate things.

"As a teacher, I think the most important thing I had to do with families was to develop relationships with them before I asked them to do anything related to school. I lived in the community. I would interact with the families of my students through the churches or the *jamaica* (festivals) with all the food booths and game booths. There are a lot of *jamaica*, usually around holidays, sometimes Hispanic holidays, sometimes American holidays. I might see the families in the grocery store or running other errands. At school, I always made sure that I chitchatted with them after school. Almost all of my students walked to school; moms came after school for them. I always went outside where the mothers were waiting. I'd play with the baby, tell a quick story about something their child had done or said, ask about other members of the family. That was the way I pulled them in to classroom.

"Then, after that, I could ask them to do something very specific that did not take much time. I had to convince them that working with their child was really important and it was something that I knew they could do. They were always worried that they were not going to be able to do what I was suggesting. I would show them exactly what to do, and reinforce that they could do what I had just shown them. Then, the mother would do it for a little while."

Case Study

This is my sixth year to teach, but my first year to teach in a predominately Hispanic school. In the classroom, I'm fine. With my colleagues, I'm fine. What is bothering me is working with these parents. At my other school, I was really good at all that family involvement stuff. Now, everything is different. Parents just do not show up at meetings. I can't seem to get any response from the letters I send home. I can't even get back the forms I send home for parents to fill out. I think it was October before I got an entire set of emergency cards for my students. I just don't get it.

Well, I guess I do understand that some of the parents don't speak English and they are probably reluctant to come to meetings. But after the first meeting when no one came, I got a translator for the next meeting. I put that in my next letter home, and still only two parents came to the next meeting. That is so frustrating. At my other school, I had family meetings at night almost every month. I had at least one parent from about 75% of my families, and now, I have to get a translator just to get two families to show up. From the first week of school, I've sent letters home every single week, telling what we are doing in class and inviting family members to join us any time they want. Not one parent has dropped in to watch what goes on in my class.

I feel like I am doing my part. In fact, I think I am doing more than my part. I am beginning to think that these parents just don't care. If they don't care, then why should I? I do not know what to do.

Response from the Hispanic Early Childhood Educator: Linda's Response to the Case Study

What stands out most in this teacher's story is in the last paragraph. She has decided that the parents of her students do not care. This may be true for one or two families in her class, but probably not for most of them. Just because they are not participating in the ways she thinks they should does not mean these parents don't care about their children or their children's education. It might be difficult for this teacher, but she needs to be less judgmental. Those families may not be coming to school because there is no one to take care of the other children. They may not come to meetings because they are worried that they will not understand everything the teacher is saying or concerned that they will not be able to put English words together so that they are understood.

Hispanic families need to feel that they are valued. English-only teachers can learn a few words and phrases in Spanish. Spanish-only parents really appreciate the fact that teachers took the time to learn something in their language. Hispanics value teachers who are accepting of their child. They are more interested in someone loving their child than they are interested in a teacher who ensures that all children in the class are making progress. And teachers need to show that they are interested in the whole family, not just the one child in their class. Hispanic parents see a good teacher as someone who is accepting of their child and is friendly to them—more so than the progress that children are making.

To be accepting of a family, you have to value their music, their food, their ways of doing things. If a teacher seems even a little apprehensive, Hispanic families just will not show up at school. They may never say anything to the teacher. They may never confront the teacher, but if negative comments are made in class, children will go home and tell their parents and the parents will never become involved in the school. One of the things Hispanic families do to show their respect for teachers is to bring them food. If they hear that the teacher does not eat the food or throws it away, they will withdraw totally.

Once Hispanic families trust a teacher, they trust teachers to be in charge of their child's education, 100%. They don't see education as something they should do. So, if teachers want Hispanic families involved, they have to work at it. They need to put out newsletters with a lot of emphasis on the children. Hispanic families get as much joy as anyone else when they see photographs or stories about their children. For any message you want to get across, use bulletin boards in the hall. Hand out articles about how children learn and how parents can help their children and how important that is, and make sure the articles are in both English and Spanish.

Characteristics of Asian Families

One Asian Early Childhood Educator and How She Describes Asian Families

 **GRACE MYONG** was born and grew up in Korea. She immigrated to the United States as a teenager and attended two years of high school, four years of college in Washington, and received a graduate degree in Michigan. Following college, Grace spent seven more years in the United States before returning to live in Korea.

"In Asian cultures, the group is more important than the individual. Rather than the individual autonomy that is seen in the United States, there is more of a sense of responsibility to the group, whether that group is a class of students, a team in the corporate world, or a family. Everyone in the group works for the benefit of the group.

"Family is critically important in Asian families; however, there is a hierarchy among family members that everyone accepts. Societal rules guide how members of the family interact with each other, even to the point of the language one uses to talk with other family members. Children are taught to respect adults and are expected to put a certain ending on verbs to show that they are speaking respectfully. Respectful language is not just expected for children speaking to adults. Brothers and sisters refer to each other by their place in the family. They use terms such as "older brother" or "younger sister" when speaking to their siblings.

"Families appear to be patriarchal, but in reality, wives run the household. The husband supports the family financially. Even in modern couples in which the husband and wife work, the husband's job is considered more important and he often

---

BOX 9.3 | *Contrasting Beliefs, Values, and Practices*

Traditional Asian Cultures	Mainstream Culture
Collective orientation	Individual orientation
Contemplative, circular thinking	Analytic, linear thinking
Tradition, living in the past	Change, future orientation
Self-denial, self-discipline	Self-assertiveness, self-gratification
Family responsibility	Individual fulfillment
Implicit, nonverbal expressions	Explicit, verbal expressions
Emotionally controlled	Emotionally expressive
Self-effacing, modest	Self-promoting, egocentric

Adapted from Lynch and Hanson, 1997

socializes with friends to further develop work relationships that could help his career. The wife works during the day and then assumes responsibility for the home as soon as she returns home in the evening. While she is working, grandparents typically take responsibility for the young children. It is not at all unusual to see three generations living together and raising the children together.

"Same-social-standing marriages are still the norm in Asian cultures, and tradition dictates that pregnancy and childbirth follow marriage quickly. The birth of a child is celebrated, with male babies more valued than females. From birth until children enter formal schooling, adults are very indulgent. Asian parents want a happy childhood for their children and deny them almost nothing. Many young children attend the equivalent of child care or preschool, and even at this level of education, many families hire tutors for four- or five-year-olds in subjects such as English, mathematics, and art. The indulgent attitude changes dramatically when children enter school.

"Beginning with the elementary grades, Asian education is rigorous. Whole-group memorization of information is valued most highly, and there is tremendous pressure for children to perform. The mother is responsible for helping the child be successful academically. The mother arranges for tutoring and works with the child herself. A child's school performance reflects back on the family and the mother is held responsible."

Case Study

I cannot believe the conference I had this afternoon after school. Ju-Hae's mother was waiting for me when I walked back into my classroom after all the other students had been picked up. She politely asked if I had a few minutes to discuss Ju-Hae. I had plans to go to the gym with a couple of friends, but I did not know this mother very well. We are only a month into school, so I haven't met with all the parents yet. I did not want to offend Mrs. Lee, so I responded that I did have time to talk.

Mrs. Lee asked how Ju-Hae was doing in my class. I talked about sorting and patterns, the math concepts we were reviewing, and what kind of work Ju-Hae was doing during math time. I pulled Ju-Hae's writing folder and talked about the progress she had made since the first day of school.

I think Ju-Hae is making good progress. I was shocked when Mrs. Lee said that this writing was not acceptable, that Ju-Hae could certainly do better work. This is first grade—only four weeks into first grade. I talked to this mother about the stages of writing and how Ju-Hae was using developmental spelling to write just about anything she wanted to write. Ju-Hae's writing is rather sophisticated for her age and experience. Mrs. Lee did not want to hear that Ju-Hae was at a higher level of writing than many children in first grade. Mrs. Lee wanted Ju-Hae to be the best.

She asked me to recommend materials she could use at home to make Ju-Hae a better reader and writer. She wants to work with Ju-Hae for two or three hours every day after school. And, on top of that, she asked for a few suggestions of good tutors. For a bright first-grader making very good academic progress, she wanted a tutor and she was going to teach Ju-Hae too.

To be honest, the whole exchange hurt my feelings. I think Ju-Hae is making good progress. Mrs. Lee does not. I think I am a pretty good first-grade teacher. Mrs. Lee does not. Now I don't know what to do. I do not think Ju-Hae needs to be spending a couple of hours a night working on school work.

Response from the Asian Early Childhood Educator:
Grace's Response to the Case Study

This exchange is a good example of a culture clash. Neither person understood the position of the other one. Mrs. Lee felt the teacher was holding her child back by not offering after-school work, while the teacher just wanted the child to be a child.

The teacher felt the mother was questioning her abilities as a teacher. This was not true. The mother was simply doing what she considered to be her duty to her child, to support her child's education. In most Asian cultures, the mother is expected to teach her child outside of school or to support educational success by enrolling her child in extra classes with a tutor. Mrs. Lee was simply asking for help in doing this. She could not praise her child's progress when the teacher shared Ju-Hae's work. It is expected in the Asian culture to remain humble about accomplishments and always expect higher levels of performance.

Teachers need to be more proactive than this teacher has been in learning about the culture of their students. Parents with different cultural backgrounds show their love and support for their children in different ways. What the teacher perceived as a demanding mother was a mother merely doing what she believed was expected of a good parent. If the teacher had understood these societal expectations, she would have interpreted the conference with Mrs. Lee very differently.

Characteristics of Native American Families

One Native American Early Childhood Educator and How She Describes Native American Families

LEISHAWN SPOTTED BEAR is a certified elementary teacher who decided to spend her career in informal education. She has worked for the Fort Worth Museum of Science and History for ten years, and currently is the assistant curator of science. Leishawn is one quarter Irish, one quarter Choctaw, and half Mandan-Hidatsa.

"It is difficult, if not impossible, to find any set of characteristics typical of Native American family life. The category itself, Native American, embraces a vast array of tribes, languages, and cultures. There is a huge variety of beliefs, customs, and physical living arrangements. Certainly the family unit is important to most, as is pride in one's tribe. Families may share their native language, speak of tribal legends, and pass on certain traditional beliefs such as

BOX 9.4 | *Contrasting Beliefs, Values, and Practices*

Native American Cultures	Mainstream Culture
Group life is most important	Life of the individual most important
Respects elders and experts	Respects youth and success
Pragmatic, accepts "what is"	Reformer, changes to "fix" problems
More emphasis how others behave than what they say	More emphasis on how others "feel" or "think"
Incorporates supportive nonfamily into family network	Keeps network of family, friends, and acquaintances separate

Adapted from Lynch and Hanson, 1997

doves being a sign of good luck or screech owls being a sign of misfortune or death, and preserve objects that are symbolic of their people. But Native American families vary tremendously, from extended families with three generations or more living under one roof, to the typical nuclear family or the single-parent household.

"My family shows just how diverse Native American families can be. I grew up in a nuclear family: mom, dad, and two kids, my sister and myself. We absorbed my father's experiences with life on the reservation; he is full-blooded Mandan-Hidatsa, a northern Plains tribe. My mother is half Irish and half Choctaw, one of the five civilized tribes of the Southeast. She came from a small town with a large Indian population.

"Within our family, my mother and father held roles that might be called traditional in any culture. He was the provider, and she took responsibility for the care of the family. She was also the disciplinarian and played a significant role in our education. Both of them wanted us to have all the opportunities that every American has. They were supportive and wanted us to be the best that we could be.

"All through school, I was one of only a handful of minorities. But I always felt included, and was normally not conscious of being Indian—at least not until I had to fill out an answer sheet for a state or national test (where I marked the box "other"), or when Thanksgiving came around, or when I saw the small paragraph in one of our textbooks on American Indians. Of both of my parents, my mother was heavily involved in our education, from helping us with our schoolwork to attending open houses, parent–teacher conferences, and extracurricular activities."

Case Study

Thanksgiving is coming up soon. I have one student in my class who is Native American. I want to ask the mother about her tribe, and if she would be willing to come in and talk about Thanksgiving from the view of a Native American, but I'm afraid of offending her. I mean, I don't know anything about the tribe.

She might be Hopi or Navaho, and her ancestors would not have lived in the Northeast where the Pilgrims settled. If that is true, then she may be upset if I bring up the subject. Also, what about the issue that the white people took their land? I want to involve the family in the life of the class, but I am not sure this is the right way to do it. I am just not sure what to do.

Response from the Native American Early Childhood Educator: Leishawn's Response to the Case Study

This teacher is worrying a bit too much. Most families would welcome a chance to share their culture and history with their child's class. There are a few Native Americans who are sensitive about the past, but chances are you will encounter many who believe in recognizing the past, but living in the present. Native Americans generally like people to ask about their tribe and what customs and traditions they still follow. This teacher should approach the mother honestly and factually. She should simply say that she is interested in having the mother share some things about her heritage with the class. If the mother feels uncomfortable being solely associated with Thanksgiving, then they can simply discuss another time.

The teacher could show that she is honoring the family's culture by asking the mother to tell an Indian legend or to share what makes their own tribe unique through foods, arts, or music.

The teacher should feel comfortable including the Native American family in other school and class events. Native Americans should not be asked to be a part of the class only when the activity is related to their culture. Native American families should be invited to do all the things that other parents are involved in: coming into the classroom to read books, going along on field trips, being a homeroom parent, and being a participant in the PTA. The teacher should just be willing to ask.

Characteristics of Middle Eastern Families

One Middle Eastern Early Childhood Educator and How She Describes Middle Eastern Families

LYDIA FERNANDEZ was born in Pakistan. Her father was born in Goa, India, which was a Portuguese colony until 1970, so Lydia's family traveled on Portuguese passports. Her education was modeled after British education. She began teaching in 1962. She married in 1969 and moved with her husband to Kuwait, where they lived until the 1990 political unrest. She taught throughout her time in Kuwait and has taught in Texas since her family immigrated to America in 1993. She is committed to accepting students where they are and teaching children in whatever ways they learn so that they are successful. Lydia offers the following explanation of Middle Eastern families.

BOX 9.5 | *Contrasting Beliefs, Values, and Practices*

Middle Eastern Culture	Mainstream Culture
Children raised to live interdependently	Children raised to live independently
Less freedom for independent learning and exploration	More freedom for independent learning and exploration
Children rarely make independent decisions	Children encouraged to make independent decisions
Respect for maturity and wisdom	Respect for youth and intelligence

Adapted from Lynch and Hanson, 1997

"Family traditions—especially male and female roles—are changing in Middle Eastern cultures, with most of the changes being influenced by the West. Western culture is everywhere in the world. Television projects Western values and American lifestyles into Middle Eastern homes, and the mindsets of those people are changing.

"Two generations ago, Middle Eastern families were more structured, with men and women having distinctly different roles. The man was the provider and the woman took care of the home and the children. The man was the senior partner and the woman deferred to his decisions. There was rejoicing at the birth of a boy, but not so with girls. Now, this is changing. Women are demanding equal opportunities because of what they have seen happening in America and in Europe. Over the past couple of decades, the attitude about male and female infants has changed so that families welcome both genders. Men are beginning to do more to support the household. With women beginning to work in Middle Eastern cities, men are beginning to take over more of the caretaking roles in the home. This is happening because the family is so valued. To keep the family closeness, both men and women are accepting new roles. In rural areas with the tribal people, the more traditional ways are still common, but these are not usually the people who immigrate to this country.

"Family is the most important unit in the Middle East. Nothing can separate the family—no quarrels, no arguments. The family is always together, and not just parents and children. Sometimes two or three generations live together and work together as family.

"Families spend time together every day in Middle Eastern families. It is common for the family to wait for dinner until every family member is home. If that happens to be 9:00 P.M., then dinner is served at 9:00 P.M. The entire family eats together, and conversation revolves around what happened to each person during the day. This is a time not only for sharing events of the day, but for adults—most often the father—to offer advice to children.

"There is more interdependence among Middle Eastern family members than in many other cultures. Not only is the extended family close, but children also stay with the family longer than do most American children. Middle Eastern children tend to live with their families until they marry. There is not a strong desire for independence from the family, such as moving out of the family home into apartments. Then, even after marriage, children tend to ask their parents for advice about issues they are considering as a couple.

"This closeness is fostered from the time that children are born. Mothers tend to keep their infants near their bodies. Children are almost always with a family member. If the mother works, the grandmother cares for the young children. Children of all ages are very important in the Middle Eastern communities. Parents are truly involved with their children, especially in the children's education. Middle Eastern adults realize that the way to have a successful life is through education. Parents recognize the potential in their children and work to guide them, to encourage them to stay on the "right track." Even beyond guiding, Middle Eastern parents tend to push their children. They push them to continue the family traditions, and at the same time they push them to work hard in school and learn as much as they can.

"Middle Eastern families value education and instill that value in their children. They will save all the money they possibly can to give their children access to higher education. They will give almost anything for their children to learn English. Even the poorest people want this for their children, and might approach a teacher, promising to give as much as they have if the teacher will teach their child English.

"Teachers are viewed differently in Middle Eastern societies than they are in America. Teachers are revered. Adults expect children to respect teachers in the same way they are taught to respect parents. Children are taught to respect their teachers to the point that Middle Eastern children are taught to stand when they answer a teacher's question."

Case Study

I am a first-year teacher working in a school with a high population of students from India, Pakistan, and Kuwait. Before this year, I never met a person from one of these countries. And here I am with eight of my students from Middle Eastern families.

I am uncomfortable with these students and their families. There is such tension now about the Middle East. I find myself avoiding conversations with these families because I am afraid if they bring up any issues about the war on terrorism and how people from the Middle East are being treated, I just won't know what to say.

One of these eight students is really giving me problems. I know that class management is important. Children have to be in control so that everyone in the class can learn. But this one boy is just out of control. He is not overtly disrespectful to me, but he talks all the time, distracting other students. He is not doing the work that I ask him to do. He is pushy on the playground, so that now, other children are beginning to reject him. They don't want him playing in their games. The situation is getting worse and worse, but I am afraid that if I try to talk to his parents they will think that I am prejudiced. I don't know what to do.

Response from the Middle Eastern Early Childhood Educator: Lydia's Response to the Case Study

This is a young teacher without much experience. She does not know very much about the values that most Middle Eastern parents hold dear. I don't think she has any idea of how much support these parents will give her if she just lets them know what is happening at school.

If she calls them and asks to talk with them, and if she presents the situation factually and honestly, the parents will most likely respond very well. They are not going to jump to the conclusion that she is prejudiced. They want their child to behave appropriately at school, and they want their child to learn. They will support the teacher and do just about anything the teacher thinks is best.

It probably would have been better if this teacher had contacted the parents the first or second week of school, maybe just a telephone call to introduce herself. It is never a good idea for the first contact with a family to be to report a problem, but even if this happens, the Middle Eastern parents are most likely going to respond to the teacher in a positive, supportive way.

Characteristics of Immigrant Families

One Early Childhood Educator Who Immigrated to the United States and How She Describes Immigrant Families

DIANE RAGHUBIR immigrated to the United States from Guyana, a small country in South America. She was nine years old when her family— her mother, father, two brothers, and two sisters—left their homeland. Her family of seven moved into Diane's uncle's home where two families were already living. Five months after arriving in New York City, Diane began her American education at P.S. 55. Diane completed her education in New York and Texas. She has taught prekindergarten and kindergarten for six years. Diane offers the following explanation of immigrant families.

"Typically, the first priority for families who immigrate to the United States is simply surviving in a new country. In many cases, immigrants are not able to find employment equivalent to what they had in their home countries, so money becomes a major issue. Families often struggle to generate sufficient money for the basics of life: a place to live, food to eat, and clothes to wear. Despite how they lived in their home countries, in most immigrant families both parents have to work, and often, more than one job.

"Many immigrant families live with relatives when they first arrive in the United States, so life at home is chaotic, because so many people are living in one house or apartment. Even as they are coping with new living arrangements and new costs of living, all members of an immigrant family are also making the transition between the culture they have known all their lives and a brand new culture. The adults typically want to balance learning how to live in their new country with keeping the traditions of their home country.

"Immigrant families often try to locate other people who have immigrated from their home country. Spending time with people who understand your culture and traditions can be very comforting.

"For school-aged children who immigrate to the United States, the transition is tremendous. Their parents are focused on day-to-day support of the family. They have little time to help their children adjust to their new schools. In many cases, children depend on other children to help them learn 'what to do.' Not understanding how American classrooms operate—and many times not speaking English—immigrant children are typically shy and somewhat withdrawn. They observe other children very carefully and try to figure out what they should be doing from moment to moment.

Case Study

I've been teaching three years, but this is the first time I have had a student who was a new immigrant to the United States. Chen is a pleasant child, never a problem, and I guess that is the problem. Chen is so quiet in class that I don't feel that I know him. I try to draw him out, but he is reluctant to answer any questions, even when it is just the two of us. I don't know how much math he understands or if he knows anything about the English alphabet. I am not even sure if he is understanding what I say to him. He always smiles at me when I am talking to him, but he has the same sort of smile on his face all the time, so I can't use facial expressions as a signal of whether or not he understands me.

I feel like I am operating in a vacuum. I strongly believe that assessment drives instruction, but I can't really assess what Chen knows when he won't talk to me.

I feel that I should talk to the parents, but I have only met them once, the first day Chen came to our school. We spoke very briefly that morning because the school secretary brought them into the classroom right in the middle of our morning routine. But it was obvious that their English was very rudimentary. I am not sure how much they would understand if I did have a conference with them, or if they would be able to do anything about Chen not talking at school. I just do not know what to do.

Response from the Early Childhood Educator Who Immigrated to This Country: Diane's Response to the Case Study

One important thing a teacher can do for immigrant parents, especially if they do not speak English, is make them feel welcome. Teachers should always greet them. Smiles go a long way in letting someone know that you value them. Smiles and gestures can communicate an invitation to parents to come into the classroom to spend some time with their child and new classmates.

One more thing that is important to remember when working with immigrant families is to find out something about their culture. Teachers don't mean to insult the parents of their students, but they can without meaning to. I remember when I first started to school in New York City, the lunch monitor made me take a bite of the school lunch. It was a hamburger. It was against my religion to eat beef, but I couldn't tell her. I was too shy. I am sure she was concerned about me getting hungry that afternoon, but she made me do something against my family's religion. She never made me do that again, but it wasn't because she learned anything about my family. I threw up when I was chewing that bite of hamburger. She never forced me to eat another thing.

Knowing a few things about a child's culture shows that teachers value their students and the families. Another thing teachers can do to show that they value immigrant families who do not speak English is learn a few words or phrases in that family's home language. Learning how to say "good morning" or "how are you doing" will not allow an entire conversation with that family, but they will appreciate the fact that the teacher is trying to communicate with them.

Teachers can also arrange for a translator to facilitate conversations. If the school district does not provide translators, a teacher could ask another parent or an older student in the school to be in the classroom a morning a week to translate brief welcoming conversations, or during family meetings or parent–teacher conferences.

If at all possible, teachers should send home written information in the families' primary language. This takes more time than translating verbal conversations, so it may not be practical to translate every piece of written information sent home. Still, non-English speaking families deserve to know as much about the life of their child's class as any other family.

Teachers should try to communicate with immigrant families as much as possible. Communicating may not be easy, but it is important. Immigrant parents want their children to be successful in school and are usually willing to do whatever it takes. But many times, immigrant families do not know what to do to support their children's learning. If the teacher lets them know what the child needs to work on at home, parents make the time to do those things, especially when the teacher provides the necessary learning materials.

The most important thing to remember when working with immigrant families or families who do not speak English is to respect them as people. If teachers respect parents, the vast majority of parents will treat teachers with respect.

Summary

A family's cultural background affects how they live, what they value, and what they believe. Many of these values and beliefs are easily identified. Some are so ingrained that people are unaware of how their culture affects them. Teachers recognize that cultural differences exist between themselves and the families of their students and work to minimize these differences.

 **Reflections**

1. Consider your own culture and how it affects your values. Make notes about your own cultural values.
2. Think about how the cultural values you identified above might come in conflict with values of other cultures.

 Field Experiences

1. Share the list of characteristics of families from one of the cultural groups discussed in this chapter with a member of that cultural group. Ask that person about perceptions of the list's accuracy.
2. Interview two or three teachers. Ask them to describe a specific time when they had a conflict related to culture with the family of one of their students and explain how they handled the situation.

 Other Activities

1. In small groups, go back through the lists of contrasting beliefs, values, and practices of different cultures. Consider how these contrasting beliefs might cause misunderstandings between families and teachers of different cultures.

 **Further Readings**

Bruns, D.A., & Corso, R. M. (2001). *Working with culturally & linguistically diverse families.* ERIC Reproduction Document Number 455972.

This ERIC Digest presents research-based strategies for working with families from diverse cultural and linguistic backgrounds. After discussing the importance of developing relationships between teachers and the families, the Digest suggests the following strategies for working with families: (1) respect the uniqueness of each family system; (2) develop a personalized relationship with families; (3) communicate in culturally appropriate ways; (4) recruit staff who view diversity as an asset; (5) create alliances with cultural guides; and (6) evaluate process and outcomes.

Chavkin, N. F., & Gonzalez, D. L. (1995). *Forging partnerships between Mexican American parents and the schools.* ERIC Reproduction Document Number 388489.

This Digest examines barriers to parent participation in the education of Mexican American students, and successful programs and strategies for overcoming those barriers. The authors suggest that the attitudes and practices of teachers and principals make a difference in the amount of parental involvement and in the achievement of students.

Dresser, N. (1996). *Multicultural manners: New rules of etiquette for a changing society.* New York: John Wiley and Sons.

Dresser offers explanations for cultural traditions and beliefs about a number of issues, from the meaning of yellow flowers in a bouquet to the opposing views about the significance of salt.

ERIC Clearing House on Urban Education. (2001). *Latinos in school: Some facts and findings.* ERIC Reproduction Document Number 449288.

Statistics about Hispanic students, preschool through college, are summarized in this summary from "Latinos in Education," a report by the White House Initiative on Educational Excellence for Hispanic Americans.

Espinosa, L. M. (1995). *Hispanic parent involvement in early childhood programs.* ERIC Reproduction Document Number 382412.

Successful early childhood programs that work with Hispanic parents recommend the following strategies: (1) a personal touch that includes personal meetings and home visits; (2) nonjudgmental communication; (3) perseverance on the part of teachers in maintaining parents' involvement; (4) bilingual support; (5) administrative support; (6) staff development activities focused on Hispanic culture; and (7) community outreach efforts in which schools and programs serve as resource and referral agencies to support families. Each strategy is discussed in this article.

Hale-Benson, J. (1986). *Black children: Their roots, culture, and learning styles.* Baltimore, MD: Johns Hopkins University Press.

This book makes the case that African American children have a relational style of learning and emotive communication style that are important parts of the African American community's legacy, tradition, and learning style.

Ladson-Billings, G. (1997). *Dreamkeepers: Successful teachers of African-American children.* San Francisco: Jossey-Bass.

As a result of her ethnographic research, Ladson-Billings describes teachers who are particularly effective working with African American children. She describes different strategies of culturally relevant pedagogy and how these strategies can be incorporated into today's classrooms.

Lynch, E. W., & Hanson, M. J. (Eds.). (1997). *Developing cross-cultural competence: A guide for working with children and their families,* 2nd ed. Baltimore: Paul H. Brookes.

Gathering information from contributors who are members of the cultural groups they discuss, Lynch and Hanson offer facts about the influence of culture on people's beliefs, values, and behaviors; descriptions of the challenges families may have adapting to a different culture; and strategies for fostering respectful and effective interactions. The book includes Anglo-European, Native American, African American, Latino, Asian, Philipino, Native Hawaiian and Pacific Island, and Middle Eastern heritages.

Lee, G. L., & Manning, M. L. (2001). Treat Asian parents and families right. *Education Digest, 67,* 39–46.

This article suggests several ways teachers can work with Asian parents and families. It also addresses the effect of language barriers on parent–teacher relationships, the importance of

nonverbal communication to Asian parents, and aspects of effective parent-education programs for Asian families.

Little Soldier, L. (1997). Is there an "Indian" in your classroom? Working successfully with urban Native Americans. *Phi Delta Kappan, 78,* 650–653.

To understand urban Native American students more fully, teachers need to understand the influence of rural/reservation living on urban life for these students and their families. Teachers should also recognize Native American students' preferred learning styles and differing sense of time.

Marshall, N. L., Noonan, A. E., McCartney, K., Marx, F., & Keefe, N. (2001). It takes an urban village, *Journal of Family Issues, 22,* 163–183.

This article describes a study that examined the extent to which an urban village exists, in a sample of African American, European American, and Hispanic American families with an elementary-school-aged child. Parental characteristics associated with the behavioral problem and social competence in children are discussed.

Riggs, S., & Dunn, R. (1996). *Hispanic American students and learning styles.* ERIC Reproduction Document Number 393607.

This ERIC Digest summarizes several research studies that examine the learning styles of most Hispanic students. These studies suggest that: (1) cool temperatures and formal design are important for Mexican American students; (2) Mexican Americans require a higher degree of structure than do other groups; (3) Mexican American students prefer solitary learning less than do Caucasian students; (4) Latinos' strongest perceptual strength is kinesthetic; and (5) Mexican American students are more field dependent than are nonminority students. The authors caution the reader that Hispanic students are a diverse group and each individual should be evaluated to determine his or her particular learning style.

Schwartz, W. (1999). *Arab American students in public schools.* ERIC Reproduction Document Number 429144.

This Digest reviews ways to provide Arab Americans with a supportive school environment, and all students with an accurate and unbiased education about the Middle East. Arab culture should be integrated into content, and teachers should review all materials to ensure the accuracy of representations of Arabs. Schwartz suggests that teachers accommodate the individuality of Arab families by taking the lead from students and their parents about school and other issues related to the student.

Tatum, B. D. (1997). *Why are all the black kids sitting together in the cafeteria? and other conversations about race.* New York: Basic Books.

The focus of this book is adolescents and racism, but Tatum's descriptions of the subtleties of racism that still exist in today's American institutions help the reader understand more deeply issues of racism.

10

Working through Other Differences between Teachers and Families

FAMILY

TEACHERS

COMMUNITY

Learning Objectives

The reader will learn and be able to discuss potential differences between teachers and families related to:

- Beliefs about educational issues
- Differences because of socioeconomic status
- Linguistic differences
- Teachers responsibilities in working through these differences

Preventing and resolving the differences that may

arise between parents, teachers, and children

with constructive communication, respect, grace, and

good humor can help make school a pleasant place.

—Lilian Katz, 1996

The previous chapter discussed cultural differences among groups of people. However, differences among people include many factors beyond culture. Teachers often deal with differences in beliefs about educational practices, differences because of socioeconomic status, and linguistic differences.

Differences in Beliefs about Educational Practices

When families send their first child to school, the only educational experiences they have against which to evaluate their child's first teacher are their own experiences. Educational practices for young children have changed since many parents were in preschool or elementary school themselves. Many parents conjure up the image of classrooms with desks in straight rows and silent children writing in individual workbooks. If this is what they knew as children, this is most likely what they view as "good education." When they do not see what they expect in their child's class, there is often a conflict between their expectations and the realities of their child's class. Whether these parents merely think about the differences, talk to other parents about their thoughts, or confront the teacher, teachers can expect to differ in educational beliefs from some of the families of their students. Following is the story of one teacher's experiences with differences in educational beliefs.

Case Study

I graduated last May with a master's degree in early childhood education, and a minor in reading. This is my first year to teach. The school is a suburban school with more parent involvement than I expected based on what I learned in my college classes. Right now, I am not sure that parent involvement is all that good a thing.

The mother of one of my students is being a real problem. She is talking behind my back, complaining to other parents in my class about how I teach. She thinks I should have reading groups like when she was in school. She thinks that the children should be working in workbooks. And, she shares her opinions with just about anyone who will listen. She approaches other parents as a concerned parent, sharing that she is concerned that her daughter is not learning anything in my class, and wondering if their child is learning anything. She seems to think that she is an expert on teaching children to learn to read. She actually brought me a set of flash cards that had sight words written on them, insisting that her older son had learned to read with these flash cards. She wanted me to start using them in my class. I teach prekindergarten!

I know that I don't know everything about teaching prekindergarten, but I know a lot. After all, I have a master's degree. I know how young children learn. I know how to support children's literacy development. I don't need a bored housewife telling me how to do my job.

I am so angry with this mother that I want to just yell at her. I know I can't do that. I wouldn't do that. But I am having problems sorting out exactly what to do. I need to help her understand that her beliefs about learning to read are just wrong, and I need to stop her from talking to other parents in the parking lot. But I am in my early twenties. She is in her early forties. And one thing that make the situation even more complicated is that she is president of the PTA this year, so she has a lot of influence in the school. I can't ignore what she is doing, but I don't want to cause more problems. I keep putting off talking with her. I am just not sure how to do what I think I need to do.

Response from an Early Childhood Educator

Charlotte Sassman has taught kindergarten and first grade for more than twenty-five years. Although she teaches full-time, Charlotte also writes district curriculum; makes local, state, and national presentations; and writes journal articles and professional books.

Charlotte's Response to the Case Study

This situation is not all that uncommon. The teacher thinks she is right; the parent thinks she is right, and neither of them is talking to the other.

There are two reactions to this case. The first is how this situation could have been avoided. New teachers need to consider how parents might react to the fact that their children are in the classroom of a first-year teacher. Parents tend to watch first-year teachers more closely than they watch experienced teachers. They want what is best for their children, and may be overly concerned about a first-year teacher's ability to be a good teacher for their child.

If the teacher had tried to think from the parents' perspective instead of thinking about how qualified she thought she was—because of her master's degree—she might have avoided this situation. The teacher could have gone on the offensive with information, rather than waiting to be put in a defensive situation. She might have begun the year with weekly letters about her plans for the year, explaining why she was doing certain things. If she had explained what her goals were for her four-year-old students—and why—then parents might have had more realistic expectations for what their children would be doing in class. If the teacher had explained what she was doing to support children's literacy development—and why—then parents might been less likely to expect the same teaching practices they had experienced when they were children, or practices that their older children had experienced.

Also, by sharing a bit of personal information, the teacher could have established the beginnings of friendship between herself and the parents. Parents are naturally concerned about the kind of person their child is going to be spending time with each day. If you can make yourself more of a real person—with likes and dislikes, hobbies and interests—then the parents seem to accept you as a competent teacher. In the absence of true information, people make assumptions. The teacher could have avoided some of the assumptions this mother was making by sharing more information sooner.

But, since this situation has occurred, the teacher needs to deal with it. The longer the situation is ignored, the harder it may be to work through it. The teacher needs to talk to the mother. In as relaxed an atmosphere as possible—perhaps over a cup of coffee and a muffin— the teacher needs to acknowledge the mother's concerns. As factually as possible, the teacher needs to share information about four-year-olds: how they learn best, the importance of all the developmental domains, and the types of experiences that support children's development. It would help if the teacher shared a book or a few articles that reinforce how she teaches. Then over the next few weeks, the teacher could extend invitations to come into the classroom to observe the children in different learning experiences, inviting all the parents, not just this mother. Then, as children are working, the teacher could explain the learning occurring in the different activities.

Differences in Socioeconomic Status

The vast majority of teachers are from the middle class. Their values have been shaped by their middle-class experiences. Many have never spent time with people who live in poverty. They may not even realize that people in different socioeconomic classes have had different life experiences which may have shaped different values. These differences in values may affect how families and teachers interact, perhaps even at a subconscious level.

Characteristics of Families Who Live in Poverty

Families who live at or below the poverty line have one primary focus in their lives: getting through the day. Most of their efforts relate to getting enough food for their

---

BOX 10.1 | *Contrasting Beliefs, Values, and Practices*

Poverty Culture/Values	Middle-Class Culture/Values
Money is to be spent	Money is to be managed
Clothing valued for style and expression of personality	Clothing valued for its quality; label important
The present is most important	The future is most important
Believes in fate	Believes in choice
Driving force is survival and relationships	Driving force is work and achievement

Adapted from: Payne, 1995

children and putting together enough money to pay rent and other household bills at the end of the month.

Living day-to-day affects how families interact. Many of these families have several children and are headed by a single mother. Sheltering and protecting young children is often a luxury that people of poverty cannot provide. Young children in these families take on more caretaking responsibilities than other children their age. Children as young as five or six years old take care of younger siblings by feeding them and supervising them. Children living in poverty are often very street smart because of the responsibilities they are expected to assume.

Of course, there are those parents who are so caught up in drugs or alcohol that they do not care for their children. The costs of their addictions can force the family into a lower socioeconomic status if they spend money to purchase drugs and alcohol for themselves instead of buying groceries or clothing for the family. These adults are focused on meeting their own needs rather than meeting the needs of their children. Because of their skewed priorities and the effects of drugs and alcohol on their decision making, most children in these families are not cared for as young children should be, and abuse and neglect are common in these families. Although many families affected by addictions do live in poverty, most people who live in poverty are not driven by drugs or alcohol. Most families living in poverty are doing the best they can for themselves and their children.

People living in poverty usually value people and relationships more than they value possessions. However, they generally view money differently than do middle-class families. When people who do not have enough money get money, they tend to make decisions about that money in the most immediate terms. Rather than save the money, they may choose to buy things to make family members or friends happy for that day. Many of these families make decisions based on the moment, rather than on the possible long-term benefits for the family.

For the most part, people living in poverty want a better life for their children, but many are not sure that that is possible. Some see school only as a place for children to go during the day, not as a place for learning; they do not recognize how education can change their lives. However, many do see education as the way for a better life and trust teachers to teach their children. They see the teacher as the educated one, the one who knows how to teach children. They see their job as feeding, clothing, and getting their children to school, not as teaching their children. A lot of teachers see that as indifference, but it is not. These families care for and about their children. They just don't come to the school. The school environment is not a place where they feel particularly comfortable.

Case Study

This is my first year to teach, and my first time to be around people who are really poor. All of my students are on the free- or reduced-lunch program, so I know that they are all living at the poverty level.

There is one thing I just don't get about the families of my students. I do not understand the way they spend money. In the first week of school, less than half of my students brought in school supplies. I didn't think it was fair that some of the students had new crayons and new markers and the others had nothing. I figured that the families just did not have enough money to buy the supplies we asked for. So, I went to the office supply store and bought boxes of crayons and markers for all the children who did not bring in their own. I also bought pencils, glue, and pencil boxes.

Early in the year, one of the other teachers gave me the idea of audio taping first-graders once a month to document their progress in reading. I thought about asking each family to send in one audio tape that I would give back to them at the end of the year. But considering what happened with school supplies, I didn't even ask them. I just went back to the office supply store and bought twenty-four audio tapes. In the second week of school I had already spent $150 in school supplies for my students. I didn't mind. I was not making a large salary, but I really didn't mind. I felt that I was providing things that my students needed.

But then, the week after Labor Day, three of my students came to school wearing new clothes, designer clothes, and those three were among the students who did not bring school supplies to school. It struck me. I can't afford designer clothes, but I was the one buying supplies for these students. They wore new clothes that entire week. How could those parents afford four new outfits for their children and not be able to buy a box of crayons and a box of markers?

Then, about a month into school, we had a wild rumpus party. We read *Where the Wild Things Are* and decided to have a wild rumpus party just like the wild things. I sent an invitation to all the families and asked them to join us at the end of the day for this party. In the invitation, I asked that they send something to eat for the party, if they could. That day, I could not believe it. Several children brought in those large bags of chocolate bars. When I'm at the grocery store, I don't buy candy. That is a luxury, and I only budget grocery money for necessities.

I feel like I want to say something, or maybe put something in my next letter to them, about how they shouldn't send expensive candy to class. We need school supplies more than we need lots of candy, but I don't know what to do.

Response from an Early Childhood Educator

Kathey Ignacio is an early childhood educator who has taught young children for more than twenty-five years. For fifteen of those years, she taught first grade in an inner city school where 90% of the students were on the free- or reduced-lunch program.

Kathey's Response to the Case Study

It would not be a good idea for this teacher to share her thoughts about how the families of her students spend their money. The teacher believes that some of the families of her students are not spending their money wisely, but this is a value judgment. If the teacher wants to have any relationship with families, if she wants to help them in any way, she cannot let them know that she judges them or how they live.

In many cases, families living in poverty make decisions based on the moment. Consider the example of the child who brings expensive candy to a school party. The teacher sees that as a poor use of money. She sees that the family has so many needs and considers the candy as luxury, not a need. On the other hand, the mother sees her child as not having all the things that the child wants or that she wants to give to the child. She may have a few extra dollars at the moment and sees the candy as one way the child can get what he wants and have some degree of status among his friends, even if it is just this one time.

The value system of people in poverty is different from that of most teachers who are middle class. These teachers must be very careful not to judge people who live by different values. The minute a teacher lets parents know that she thinks they are making bad decisions is the minute that she stops having any positive influence on that family. It is difficult, in many cases, to keep opinions to yourself, but that is absolutely necessary when working with families who hold different values.

Linguistic Differences

To state that not all families speak English is quite obvious; however, many educators do not think about what it will be like when they have families in their classes who speak other languages. Communication is difficult with people who speak a different language, but is very hard when a teacher wants to talk with a family about their child.

Characteristics of Families Whose Home Language Is Not English

Families who speak a language other than English are as varied as families in the general population. Among these families, there are differences in cultural beliefs and traditions, differences in socioeconomic status, differences in gender roles, and differences in family expectations for children. Despite all these differences, families whose primary language is not English do have some similarities.

When parents do not speak the primary language of the school, they tend to live in more isolation than they would if they could communicate with most people in that environment. They tend to spend time with people who share their language and avoid encounters with people who speak only English.

Parents who do not speak English tend to avoid their child's teacher and the school in general. Unable to communicate to be understood by English-only educators, they often stay away from the school. They are uncomfortable trying to communicate with gestures and possibly a few words or phrases.

Case Study

I grew up only hearing English spoken. I don't think I even heard a different language spoken until I was in high school and took a Spanish class. I tried to learn Spanish, but I am not very good at hearing and learning other languages. Now, here I am in a school where parents speak six languages other than English. Out of twenty students, half of them speak English as a second language. They are all at different points of English fluency. Some of them are still using simple phrases to communicate, while others speak standard English with only a slight accent. But their parents are a different matter. None of the parents in these ten families speak English well enough to hold a conversation about what we are doing at school, their children, or their children's progress.

That puts me in a terrible position. I feel that I only communicate with half of the families of my students. This is not fair to the families. I know that. But I have ten families and six languages to deal with, and I don't know where to start.

Response from an Early Childhood Educator

Tara Teague was trained as an early childhood educator, but has chosen to teach fourth grade in Birdville Independent School District in North Richland Hills, Texas, for the past five years. She uses all the early childhood teaching strategies she learned to create child-centered learning experiences for her students. She is now working on a master's degree in counseling, which also gives her insight into working with her students and their families.

Tara's Response to the Case Study

This is not an easy position for this teacher. It is very frustrating to want to communicate with people and not be able to do that. What she needs to remember is that these families also want to talk with her, and they feel the same sense of frustration that she feels. They are frustrated by not being able to communicate with the person who spends so much time with their child. But they also feel that frustration with lots of other people in their lives. So, families who do not speak English are more frustrated with more people more of the time than the teacher is. If she tries to understand their perspective, she will be much more inclined to search out resources that can help her communicate with these families.

The most important step in communicating with these families is finding a translator. That is easier said than done, but in most cases, if the teacher talks with enough people, she can find people to serve as translators. The most obvious place to begin looking is among families within the school. Next, teachers should contact school district personnel for assistance. Third, older students in the school could be used to translate greetings from the teacher to the families and simple information about the class, although students should not be used to translate information that would be considered confidential. Finally, there may be community organizations or agencies willing to provide these services or help find an individual who can come to the school to translate between the teacher and a family, or translate written communication from a teacher to families.

Another thing a teacher in this position might consider is organizing family time in the class in which children share with their families. In this case, children might be explaining what they do during math time or sharing different books the class has read. During this type of event, non-English-speaking families would see that others are in their same position and might be less reluctant to join the class at other times. On the teacher's part, smiles and welcoming gestures go a long way in making people feel less uncomfortable. If possible, learning a phrase or two in each language would show families that she is reaching out to them.

Educators' Responsibilities in Working through Differences with Families

When there are misunderstandings between families and teachers, both parties have to be willing to work through the differences. However, the reality of these situations is that the teacher must be the one to initiate conversations with families. Teachers must reach out to families and take the lead in working through differences.

The best-case scenario is that teachers begin developing relationships with families from the beginning of the school year. When teachers take the time to introduce themselves to families and ensure that families feel comfortable in the classroom and at school, families are likely to respond to these welcoming gestures. Likewise, when teachers take the time and expend the effort to keep families informed, most parents appreciate the effort and become more open with teachers. When teachers create specific times to share with families, it gives both teachers and families opportunities to get to know one another.

Many potential conflicts may be prevented through the teacher's proactive efforts to involve family members. Even when problems do arise, it is easier to work through differences when there is a relationship already established between a teacher and the families of her students.

The early childhood educators responses to the case studies presented in this chapter (and the previous chapter) included similarities in what each teacher said:

- ☑ Learn about the cultures of the families of students.
- ☑ Get to know families early in the year.
- ☑ Treat families with respect.
- ☑ Invite families to class/school for nonthreatening opportunities to learn more about their children.
- ☑ Keep families informed about the life of the class.

Taking these actions and establishing relationships with families requires time and effort on the part of the teacher. However, the investment of time and energy definitely pays off when differences or conflicts develop between a teacher and the family of a student.

 **Summary**

Differences exist among individuals within any group. Differences exist between families and teachers in socioeconomic status, language, culture, and beliefs about education practices. When teachers are aware of possible differences, they can take steps to prevent many potential misunderstandings.

 **Reflections**

1. Imagine yourself as a parent living in a country where English is not the predominant language. Consider how you might feel about visiting your child's classroom, having conversations with the teacher, and attending parent meetings.

2. Read the first article listed under Further Readings for this chapter, "If you can pass Momma's tests, then she knows you're getting your education: A case study of support for literacy learning within an African American family." Consider how this article presents how low-income, African American families value education compared with your perceptions before reading this article.

Field Experiences

1. Interview two or three teachers. Ask them to describe a specific time when they had a conflict related to educational beliefs with the family of one of their students and explain how they handled the situation.
2. Interview two or three teachers. Ask them to describe a specific time when they had a conflict related to socioeconomic differences with the family of one of their students and explain how they handled the situation.
3. Interview two or three teachers. Ask them to describe a specific time when they had a conflict related to linguistic differences with the family of one of their students and explain how they handled the situation.

Other Activities

1. Make a list of things that might make you feel more comfortable in the imagined situation of Reflection #1. File this list so that it can be easily retrieved if you find yourself teaching children whose home language is not English.
2. In small groups, read the ERIC Digest article by Lilian Katz, "Preventing and resolving parent–teacher differences" and discuss with the group how her suggestions for the teacher's role in parent participation programs could be implemented.

Further Readings

Baumann, J. F., & Thomas, D. (1998). "If you can pass Momma's tests, then she knows you're getting your education": A case study of support for literacy learning within an African American family. *The Reading Teacher, 51,* 108–120.

This article shares information about education, literacy learning, and the roles of parents and teachers in supporting children's achievement from two different roles, that of teacher and that of single-parent, low-income, African American mother.

Bess, S. (1994). *Nobody don't love nobody: Lessons on love from the school with no name.* Placerville, CA: Goldleaf Press.

Bess tells her own story of teaching homeless children in a shelter-based school. The vignettes about her students and their families give the reader a glimpse into the challenges homeless adults with children face.

Bracey, G. W. (2001). School involvement and the working poor. *Phi Delta Kappan, 82,* 95–96.

This article discusses parents' availability for school participation, determining that work-related factors such as income and vacation benefits contribute to wide variance in family involvement.

Bullough, R. V., Jr. (2001). *Uncertain lives: Children of promise, teachers of hope.* New York: Teachers College Press.

Bullough shares the stories of thirty-four children who face daily challenges of poverty, drug abuse, and absent fathers. Rather than present the stories in a way that elicits sympathy for the children, Bullough connects their stories to the larger issues that schools and society must address.

Katz, L. G. (1996). *Preventing and resolving parent-teacher differences.* ERIC Reproduction Document Number 401048.

Parents and teachers share responsibility for creating a working relationship that fosters children's learning. This Digest examines the cultural context for parent–teacher relationships, suggests some general strategies for creating a climate in which misunderstandings and disagreements between parents and teachers can be minimized through communication, and discusses some general principles for parents and teachers in dealing with disagreements as they arise.

Kotlowitz, A. (1992). *There are no children here: The story of two boys growing up in the other America.* New York: Random House.

Kotlowitz's experience as a journalist shows through this true story about Pharoh and Lafeyette Horner who are growing up in a project in Chicago. Hiding during drive-by shootings, avoiding drug dealers, and dealing with gangs are presented as the everyday events that they are in the lives of these boys. Kotlowitz portrays their lives in such detail and description that the reader feels a part of Pharoh's and Lafeyette's family.

Kozol, J. (1992). *Savage inequalities: Children in America's schools.* New York: HarperCollins.

As an advocate for children who live in poverty and attend the nation's poorest schools, Kozol exposes schools in East St. Louis, Chicago, New York, Washington, DC, New Jersey, and San Antonio. He reveals the inequalities that exist between urban schools and inner-city schools. Children of poverty endure outdated textbooks, overcrowded classrooms, classes held in closets, holes in ceilings, and roofs so old that it rains in classrooms.

Martinez, Y. G., & Velazquez, J. A. (2000). *Involving migrant families in education.* ERIC Reproduction Document Number 448010.

This article describes family involvement from the perspectives of migrant parents and teachers. It helps teachers understand how migrant parents view education and their role in it, and offers strategies to enhance the experience of schooling for migrant students and their families.

11

Getting Started with Family Involvement and Moving into the Community

FAMILY
TEACHERS
COMMUNITY

Learning Objectives

The reader will learn and be able to discuss:

- Their own plans for working with families
- How they will implement family involvement plans
- Ways to involve the community in the life of a class/school

When it comes to improving student achievement, not all parent-involvement activities are created equal. While school officials are enthusiastic about recruiting parents as volunteers, they should be aware that the cookie-baking, word-processing, candy-selling, paper-shuffling, showing-up activities traditionally associated with parent involvement are not likely to have much impact on student achievement.

—Rebecca Jones, 2001

Making Plans for Family Involvement

The previous five chapters describe many strategies that can be used to encourage family involvement and many issues that might bring about conflict between teachers and families.

All of the issues discussed in Chapters 6 through 10 are factors to consider when planning and implementing a family involvement program. Each strategy for working with families has its own advantages and disadvantages. Some are more time-consuming than others. Some require more resources than many classroom teachers can garner without help. Each strategy appeals to different families.

Each group of families has different backgrounds and life experiences that affect how they respond to the various family involvement strategies. It is important to think about the specific group of families when planning the family involvement program to implement in a classroom.

There are many factors to consider in planning a family involvement program, but perhaps the most important point to remember is to start small. It would be a mistake to try to implement all of the strategies discussed in Chapters 6, 7, and 8 at the same time. It is better to start with one or two strategies and be successful, than to try too many things at the same time and not be able to keep up with each strategy. If a teacher tells families that she will send a letter home every week, she needs to live up to that promise. Missing every other week because life gets too busy will negatively affect how families feel about the teacher. However, if she tells families

VOICES *of Teachers*

After talking to several experienced teachers, I decided for my first year of teaching to tell the families of my students that I would write to them once a week to let them know what was going on in the class and that I would have a family meeting once every six weeks. Of course, I talked to as many parents as I could when they came to the classroom, but I thought that writing the letters and having the meetings would be about as much as I could handle that first year. As it turned out, I was wrong. It really didn't take that much time to do these two things, so after the winter break, I added phone calls to my list of family involvement strategies. I called one or two families every day. They were just quick calls to say something positive about their child. Then after spring break I decided to plan a family art night. It was such a success, and families were so supportive, that together we planned a family field trip to the fire station and another family night where the students read books and recited poetry. I feel like I got very close to the families of my students. Next year, I am planning to do even more things with families.

Teachers need time to plan family involvement strategies.

at the beginning of the school year that she will keep them informed by sending home a newsletter every month, yet she finds herself sending the newsletter home every other week, the families will be pleasantly surprised. In both cases, the teacher is sending home the same amount of information in the same time frame, but one teacher is perceived negatively, and the other is perceived positively. It is important to live up to commitments made to families.

Anytime a person begins doing something new, that task usually takes longer than it does after it becomes routine. Teachers implementing family involvement strategies find this is no different. When teachers first begin to write family letters, it may take three or four hours to decide what to write, draft the letter, and revise it so that the language is at the appropriate reading level and sounds as warm and friendly as desired. However, after a month or two of writing letters to the same group of families, the time required may be down to less than an hour. The first time a teacher plans an event night for the families in her class such as a family math night, it might take an hour or two every day for two weeks to make sure that everything is well planned and implemented so that everyone has a good time and learns something meaningful. After one event like this, the planning for the next one is more than cut in half.

Each teacher should make her own decisions about which family involvement strategies to implement in any given year. Deciding on methods of communication and strategies for shared time depends on the schedule of the teacher and the preferences of the families with whom she is working that particular year.

Implementing Plans for Family Involvement

Returning to the comments of teachers in Chapter 3, it is common to feel apprehensive about beginning to work with families in new ways. Reaching out to the families of students, interacting with a large number of virtual strangers, requires a certain amount of risk-taking. But considering the benefits of family involvement, it is certainly worth taking the risk and investing the time. Both the families and the teacher receive positive benefits from the communications.

Whatever strategies a teacher decides to implement, it is important to remember to create the impression of being open and easy to approach. When family members feel they are welcome in the classroom, they are more likely to spend time there. When they feel the teacher is interested in them, they are more likely to talk with the teacher.

When a teacher begins implementing components of a family involvement plan, families may be reluctant to respond. It is important not to give up on plans for family involvement if, at first, the strategies do not seem to be working out as planned. Many families have never been involved in their children's education before their child entered your class. Teachers need to give families time to get used to a new way of thinking about being involved in school events and working with their children at home. If families do not immediately respond to weekly informative letters, a teacher should keep sending them. Over time, when families recognize a teacher's commitment to keeping them informed, they are more likely to respond.

Family members will spend time in the classroom when they feel comfortable there.

If families do not come to evening family meetings or event nights, a teacher should keep having them on a regular basis (and ask families who attend to call and invite other families to come to the next one). Over time, more families will attend the meetings. When families do not respond at first, keep remembering the benefits of family involvement. Teachers need to keep reaching out to families and believe that, over time, the time and effort invested pays off with responses from the families.

It helps to reread books and journal articles that describe the benefits of family involvement. When reminded of the great benefits for all parties, even teachers who have become discouraged about the initial responses to their efforts can be reenergized and decide to keep reaching out to families in every way that they possibly can. Another helpful strategy is to find support from another teacher who is reaching out to families. Trading ideas and talking over problems with a colleague benefits both parties. Over time and with consistent implementation of family involvement strategies, most families will respond and become involved at some level.

Working in and with the Community

Once a number of families are involved in a class or in the school, teachers can begin to look beyond immediate family members and consider involving other people in the community. Informal community involvement can be encouraged by seeking out individuals who have some indirect interest in the school. More formal community involvement can be fostered through seeking out corporations or other community organizations that might be interested in supporting education-related efforts.

Informal Community Involvement

Informal community involvement generally refers to individuals who do things for a school because they have some connection to the school or who volunteer at the school because of some commitment to education. These individuals are often extended family members of students, friends of these families, friends or family of faculty, retired educators, or people who live very close to the school.

FRIENDS OF SCHOOL FAMILIES   Each family in a class or in a school has friends and extended family members. These people are also potential candidates for volunteers within the school. The more involved families become, the more they are invested in the school. As they become aware of the school's needs, they are often willing to ask their friends and families to help the school.

Networking through the families of students to reach their friends and other family members can identify other people who are willing to help out in the school when asked. This assistance could take many forms. Here are only a few examples of community resources committed to an elementary school because the parents of students in that school asked other people to consider donations of time or other things:

- ☑ The friend of a parent owned a printing firm. When asked, he donated all kinds of paper stock and envelopes to the elementary school.
- ☑ The friend of another parent donated carpet squares from discontinued lines to different classes of the school.
- ☑ A teacher mentioned to one mother that she would like to have a construction center in the kindergarten class, but did not have time to collect the necessary items. This mother talked to other families in the class and asked them to talk to their friends and family members. In less than two weeks, people brought in scrap wood, balsa wood, paper towel rolls, plastic tubing, pieces of PVC pipe, different kinds of tape, wood glue and school glue, small nails, and tools. The construction center was a huge success with the students, and family members and friends of the school made it happen.
- ☑ Students in one class decided in October to begin saving empty egg shells so they could make confetti eggs for a spring festival. Over the weeks, children and their parents asked friends and family members to help them save eggs. By the week of the spring festival, more than 50 families had donated 218 dozen empty eggs. When sold for $. 25 each, this class made $650. They decided to spend the entire amount on books for their class library.
- ☑ After reading Steven Kellogg's book, *How Much is a Million?*, one class decided to collect tabs from aluminum cans. They wanted to see what a million tabs looked like. It took two years and the help of dozens of friends and family members, but they did it (by the way, 100,000 tabs fit nicely in a 30-gallon trash can).
- ☑ The aunts and uncles of one student spent two Saturdays painting the cafeteria, complete with a mural on one wall.
- ☑ When asked by parents of one elementary school, fifty-three local businesses gave gift certificates or small gifts to the school's silent auction. From these gifts alone, the school made $2,500 in the silent auction. These funds were used for field trips for students.

FRIENDS AND FAMILY OF TEACHERS   Just as friends and relatives of families of a school can often be encouraged to support different volunteer opportunities, so can friends and family members of the faculty and staff. Some teachers are, by nature, more willing to ask people they know to "help out" in their classes. A first-year teacher hired the week before school started began making phone calls within an hour of signing a contract. Within a few days, friends and family members she asked for favors volunteered to

- ☑ Sew curtains for the classroom windows
- ☑ Make pillows for the reading center
- ☑ Build bookshelves and a reading loft

VOICES *of Teachers*

We didn't have any equipment on the playground at school. The children brought toys to play with, but that did nothing for their physical development. I brought this up at one of the meetings I had with my families, and I couldn't believe what happened. Two couples took what I said to heart. They got together after the meeting and talked about what could be done. A couple of days later they talked to me, and then talked to the principal. Those mothers decided that they were going to talk to other families and try to raise money for the playground. Those fathers decided they were going to talk to other families about volunteering to come to school on a few Saturdays to help build play-ground equipment. Of course, the principal approved their plans.

Over the summer, those two families made that playground happen. The mothers got donations from several families in the school and several of the businesses around the school. The fathers got families in the school and friends of those families to build the playground equipment. It was very exciting.

When we came back to school in August, the students were so happy. Some of the teachers and I had the children write thank you notes to everyone who helped with money or by volunteering. Now we are planning a dedication party and we'll invite all of those people. I think we may have taken a first step in involving people outside the school in our school.

☑ Make signs for nine learning centers
☑ Cover bulletin boards with canvas or heavy cotton fabric
☑ Donate paints and collage materials for an art center
☑ Donate rocks, fossils, and shells for a science center
☑ Go to garage sales and thrift stores and put together a cooking center, complete with hot plate, toaster oven, a mixer, bowls, measuring cups, and spoons
☑ Help arrange furniture and set up learning centers in the classroom.

More than a dozen friends and family members helped get the room ready for the first day of school, and more than half of those people got so attached to that class that they continued volunteering in the class at least once a month during the entire school year. This is just one example of what one teacher asked for and got from people she was close to. This example shows what people are often willing to do when they are asked.

RETIRED EDUCATORS Another group of people to approach for volunteering in a center or school is retired early childhood educators. Just because someone is old enough to be officially retired does not mean that he or she is no longer

Retired educators can be effective volunteers.

VOICES *of Teachers*

I was so excited about retirement. I kept thinking about sleeping as late as I wanted, eating lunch whenever I felt hungry instead of eating because that time was my class's designated lunch time, and going shopping just about any time I felt like it. And retirement was great, for about three months. Then I found myself really missing being around young children. They bring such joy to life. I love their enthusiasm. I love looking at the world from their eyes. Sure, I enjoyed my friends, but they can't provide that interaction that I had with young children when I was teaching. So I looked around, located three child care centers within a short driving distance, and visited each one of them. I chose the most child-centered program and offered to volunteer two mornings a week. The situation is great. Every Tuesday and Thursday, I read to the three-year-olds, and then do a follow-up activity. Then I work with children as they work in their learning centers. I've developed close relationships with all of those children and love the time I spend with them.

knowledgeable about young children or is not interested in working with children. When retired educators are asked to consider volunteering—especially when they are approached to become involved in a very specific way such as coming to the school two afternoons a week to tutor two or three children who are struggling in reading or math—they are often willing to do just that. Usually, acknowledgment of their expertise in working with children who need extra help and a specific request make people more than willing to agree.

PEOPLE WHO LIVE IN THE SCHOOL'S NEIGHBORHOOD   People who live near a school or center have an indirect interest simply because they are neighbors. When faculty or staff reach out to the school's neighbors and keep them informed about the life of the school on a periodic basis, they generally appreciate it. When they are invited to school events, they may attend. Over time, their general interest in the school or center can be turned into more specific interest and perhaps volunteering.

Formal Community Involvement

Informal community involvement by individuals can sometimes lead to more formal involvement in which corporations or organizations join with schools in a partnership. More and more community agencies are working with elementary schools to

Businessman and teachers work together planning formal community involvement.

provide health care and other family support services at the school site. Collaborations between schools and agencies offer benefits for both partners. Schools can provide access to families who may require the assistance of several agencies, thus maximizing equitable distribution of services while minimizing experiences and service duplication. Families who are already familiar with the school and comfortable in that setting may use agency assistance when they might otherwise procrastinate before seeking assistance. Services available at any individual school vary, but may include hearing, vision, and developmental screenings; physical and dental checkups; speech and language therapy; counseling or therapy; nutrition counseling; and assistance in completing paperwork for federal- or state-funded assistance programs. When a school works with community agencies, the families and their children benefit.

VOICES of Families

My company was looking for something to do for our city. It is just good public relations when a company gives back to the community in some way. My children attend a public school in the suburb where we live. I've always been impressed with the way that parents support that school. Any time you go to the school, there are parents working in classrooms, in the library, in the nurse's clinic, and in the office. I know that every school does not get this level of support from parents. I drive by the same elementary school every day on my way to work. It is obvious, just from looking at the outside of the school, that it isn't supported in the same ways that my child's school is. On a whim, one day I stopped at the school and asked to talk to the principal. He was a warm man who seemed very committed to the students.

Over the next few weeks, I met with that principal a couple of times, and I talked with our company's vice president. I put together a partnership between us. My company ended up "adopting" the school. At the time, we weren't sure what that would mean. We are now five years into our partnership. As a company, we've donated school supplies, purchased books for all of the students two or three times, and helped them acquire computer software that teachers said they needed. About twenty employees have volunteered to be mentors for different students. They commit to go to the school once a week and work with one child for an hour.

I feel good about our involvement in the school. We help them in lots of ways, but really those students—and teachers and administrators—give back to us just as much as we give to them. I encourage other companies in our city to do the same thing. It is just a good thing to do.

Summary

Teachers should plan and implement family involvement strategies slowly, over time, so they do not become overwhelmed. Once a strong family involvement program is in place, teachers should consider moving beyond working with the families of students and begin involving community members in the life of the school.

Reflections

1. Consider the responsibilities of a first-year teacher, then think about a family involvement program that would be both manageable in terms of the teacher's time and sufficient to attract and maintain families' interest.
2. Think about some ways to involve people in the community in the life of an elementary school.

Field Experiences

1. Schedule a meeting with a small group of officers for a local school's parent–teacher association. Talk with them about ways they try to involve families in the school and how they work to involve people in the community.
2. Interview several teachers about the factors they consider when they plan how they are going to work with the families of their students. Ask them how much their plan changes from year to year.
3. Identify a local business or corporation that encourages its employees to volunteer in elementary schools. Schedule an interview with an officer of the company about the reasons the company believes that corporate–education partnerships are important.

Other Activities

1. Draft a newsletter about a school, considering the neighbors of the school as the primary audience.
2. Draft a thank you letter to a corporation, thanking them for their involvement in a school (use the company described in the Voices of Families box on p. 152 as the audience).

3. Do an Internet search to find ways that schools/teachers involve the community in their school.

Further Readings

Christensen, B. (1996). *Building parent partnerships.* Washington, DC: National Education Association.

Christensen suggests building blocks for greater parent involvement in schools, including ways to accommodate parents' busy schedules and to address the changes in the nature of today's families, as well as planning effective parent conferences, newsletters, and much more.

Coleman, M. (1997). Families and schools: In search of common ground. *Young Children, 52,* 14–21.

This article presents a training model to guide parents and teachers in thinking through family involvement in early childhood programs, first by brainstorming ways families can be involved, and second, by creating a philosophical statement and examining roles shared by parents and teachers.

Websites to Explore

- School/Community Partnerships to Support Language Minority School Success http://www.cal.org/crede/pubs/ResBrief5. pdf

    This research brief prepared by the Center for Research on Education, Diversity, and Excellence discusses partnerships between schools and community organizations/agencies.
- A Guide to Promising Practices in Educational Partnerships http://www. ed. gov/pubs/PromPract/

    Sponsored by Educational Partnerships Program, Office of Educational Research and Improvement, U.S. Department of Education, this guide includes examples of educational and community needs assessments; approaches to recruiting partners and volunteers; staff development for social service agency, school, and business personnel; student support services, including mentors and coaches; and community involvement, including parent education and "town hall" meetings.

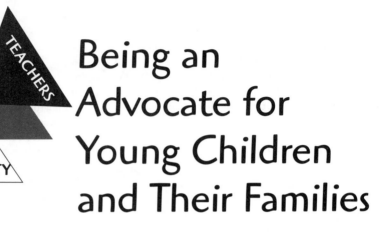

12

Being an Advocate for Young Children and Their Families

Learning Objectives

The reader will learn and be able to discuss:

- Public policy advocacy with legislatures and school boards
- Private-sector advocacy
- Personal advocacy
- Important issues for advocates to remember

> Effective advocacy, especially policy advocacy, requires vision, commitment, stamina, and optimism.
>
> —Adele Robinson and Deborah Stark, 2002

The closer teachers get to families, the more they realize the needs of families, and the more willing they are to become advocates for children and their families. Many people associate the term *advocacy* with the political arena—influencing policies that are established and laws that are enacted. Because young children have no voice in this process, early childhood educators often assume the responsibility of presenting the needs of young children and their families to the individuals and groups who set policies and pass laws. Adele Robinson and Deborah Stark (2002) refer to this type of advocacy as *public policy advocacy.* They also describe two other primary forms of advocacy as *private-sector advocacy*—trying to change corporate policies and practices to support children and their families—and *personal advocacy*—sharing personal beliefs with other individuals and groups.

Public Policy Advocacy

Public policy advocacy involves the efforts of individuals and groups to influence laws, policies, and practices of local, state, and federal legislatures, boards, and agencies. It often feels as if typical people cannot affect decisions made at such levels, but that is not true.

The people who make law and public policies do not make these decisions in isolation. These decision makers are influenced by other people. Although legislators and board members may have their own opinions on different topics, they typically make decisions based on more than simple opinion. They want solid information related to the decisions they are called on to make. Typically, their staff is responsible for gathering information related to a particular bill or policy and organizing that information.

There is no reason that early childhood educators should not be among the people who try to influence decision makers. Early childhood educators have a specialized body of knowledge related to young children and their families. This information should be shared with those making decisions about young children. Early childhood educators need to establish relationships with local, state, and federal decision makers and be willing to supply pertinent information related to bills and policies being considered. A state-level senator says, "Politics works for those who show up" (Mike Moncrief, personal communication, August 2001). Knowledgeable early childhood educators are among the people who need to "show up" when laws and policies that affect young children and their families are being shaped.

Beyond providing accurate information about specific bills and policies, early childhood educators need to assume the responsibility of helping to educate people in positions of power. The body of knowledge about young children continues to increase rather dramatically. In the past few years, neuroscience has added tremendously to the understanding of the brain development of young children. Continuing research conducted by educators, psychologists, and physicians points to environments and teaching strategies that best support the development and learning of young children. As results of this research are published, it is important that early childhood educators stay current themselves, and share that knowledge with people who are in the position of making decisions that create law or set policy affecting young children. Those who know the most about young children "must translate their knowledge and strong commitment into advocacy, working to ensure that the policies, practices, and investments made by our schools, governments, and businesses are right for our children" (Robinson and Stark, 2002, p. 5).

Advocacy efforts for young children and their families go beyond those related to education. Early childhood educators need to support bills and policies that support developmentally appropriate education for young children, but there are also many other issues that should be considered for individual or group advocacy efforts. A partial list is provided in Box 12.1.

Any of these issues can and should be supported by individual teachers. However, advocacy efforts are usually more effective when a group of like-minded individuals join together.

BOX 12.1 | *Issues Related to Young Children and Their Families*

- Abuse and Neglect
- Adoption
- After-School Programs
- Child Care, Federal Programs
- Child Care, State Programs
- Children's Health Insurance Program (CHIP)
- Dental Care
- Domestic Violence
- Early Education
- Early Head Start
- Environmental Hazards
- Food Stamps
- Foster Care
- Head Start Program
- Health Care

- Immunizations
- Infant Mortality
- Kinship Care
- Media
- Medicaid
- Mental Health
- Parental Substance Abuse
- Poverty
- Prekindergarten
- Prenatal Care
- School Safety
- Teen Pregnancy
- Temporary Assistance to Needy Families
- Violence Prevention

When a person begins to work in the area of public policy advocacy, it is easier to join the efforts of an organized group. One of the first places to look for such groups is professional educational organizations such as National Association for the Education of Young Children (NAEYC). Many professional organizations organize advocacy efforts by providing information on their websites and sending action alerts by email. Signing up to receive such information works well for national issues. However, large professional organizations rarely track state or local bills or policies. For this type of information, teachers should look for statewide organizations that track bills being proposed in a particular state's senate or house of representatives. For local information, it is usually necessary to locate a community organization. Armed with the information that organizations supply and with the encouragement they provide, early childhood educators can begin working in the political arena with confidence.

Federal and State Legislatures

Anyone who wants to influence decision making at the federal or state level first needs to learn about the processes through which laws are created. Armed with this knowledge, advocates for or against particular pieces of legislation are most effective when they

- ✓ Keep informed and stay current
- ✓ Develop a relationship with the person they are trying to influence, or with the staff of the legislator
- ✓ Are willing to provide information the representative or senator needs (or requests) related to specific areas of expertise
- ✓ Create brief materials related to a specific issue and a proposed solution (that is, effective advocates do not present problems to legislators without also being prepared to present a workable answer to that problem)
- ✓ Are visible in the process by being present at hearings, meetings in the community, and in legislators' offices

There are several ways of communicating with elected officials: telephone calls, letters, emails, or personal visits. Personal visits are usually the most effective way of influencing policy; however, they require the most commitment of time and effort. There is no obvious advantage among telephone calls, letters, and emails. Some legislators, or their staff, prefer one over the other. This is something that should be investigated when communicating with senators and representatives.

TELEPHONE CALLS   Telephone calls take only a few minutes. When teachers call a legislator, they typically speak with a legislative aide or staffer, so people should ask to speak with the person who is responsible for the topic they wish to address. It is important to keep the message rather brief: identify yourself, say that you support or oppose a particular bill (be able to identify the bill by number), give one or two reasons for your support or opposition, and ask about the legislator's position on that bill. If you are considering calling federal legislators and need the telephone number of your senator or representative, you can call the United States Capitol switchboard at (202)224-3121 and ask for your senator's and/or representative's office. Telephone numbers for state legislators can be found on state government websites or in a telephone book.

LETTERS   Letters take more time than telephone calls, but provide the opportunity to have opinions documented. Effective advocacy letters are brief, one page or less, and straight to the point. They state the purpose of the letter in the first paragraph. If the letter relates to a specific bill, that specific piece of legislation should be referenced by number. In following paragraphs, teachers should state support or opposition to the bill, and offer reasons for that position. An illustrative story can increase the letter's effectiveness.

When addressing a letter to a federal senator, this is the correct format:

The Honorable (full name)
__(Rm.#)__(name of) Senate Office Building
United States Senate
Washington, DC 20510

Dear Senator:

When addressing a letter to a federal representative, this is the correct format:

The Honorable (full name)
(Rm.#)__(name of) House Office Building
United States House of Representatives
Washington, DC 20515

Dear Representative:

When writing to the chair of a committee or the Speaker of the House, it is proper to address them as Dear Mr. Chairman or Madam Chairwoman or Dear Mr. Speaker.

EMAIL   When emailing legislators, the same guidelines for writing letters apply. Professional organizations often provide drafts of letters related to issues related to young children and their families. It is very easy—and quite tempting—to simply copy the draft letter and paste it into the body of an email and send that to a legislator. However, a number of identical emails (or letters) received by a legislator will not be viewed as strongly as the same number of emails that are personalized.

PERSONAL VISITS   Personal visits with legislators or their staff require a commitment of time that is difficult for many classroom teachers. Still, one-on-one discussions are the best way to develop relationships with individuals who work in different areas of the legislative process.

When meeting with legislators or their staff, it is important to be on time for the meeting and to remain professional throughout the meeting. Respecting the other person's time, teachers need to state their position succinctly and convey the reasons for that position.

School Boards

Public policy advocacy at the local level often occurs with school boards. These bodies enact policies that affect young children within a particular school district. The methods of contacting school board members are the same as for contacting legislators.

School boards are usually very responsive to families and their concerns. However, many families are not aware of issues that are being considered by the board or don't know how to go about expressing their opinions to board members. Teachers tend to be more aware of issues to be addressed by school board members at particular meetings. Teachers can share this information with families and encourage them to share their opinions with board members. Teachers can offer to go to school board meetings with families for support. With the support of someone they respect and trust, family members are more likely to get involved and try to influence the policies set by the school board.

VOICES *of Teachers*

I have never been involved in politics. I never wanted to be. Then a friend of mine, another teacher, asked if I would write a letter to my state representative and senator about a bill they were considering. Both houses had a bill about teacher certification. The bill basically said that anyone who had a B.A. or a B.S. in anything could become a public school teacher by taking and passing the two state standardized certification tests. These people would not have to take even one college course in child psychology or child development, no hours in educational methods of any kind. I know there is a shortage of teachers, but I wondered what these people would know about observation and assessment of children, or working up lesson plans, much less developing curriculum. It really made me mad. I have a master's degree in early childhood education and still feel that I have so much to learn about being the best early childhood educator I can be, and here were these legislators basically saying that anyone who can get a college degree knows enough about children to teach. That was my first step in advocacy for children in the political arena.

Private-Sector Advocacy

Public policy advocacy is not the only arena to influence decisions that affect young children. Private-sector advocacy attempts to influence corporate decisions that affect young children and their families. This type of advocacy can range from educating business leaders about the need to have family-friendly policies in their businesses to challenging manufacturers of children's toys so that they are safe for children of all ages.

Private-sector advocates frequently enlist business leaders to serve on community committees working on issues that affect young children and their families. Examples of issues these committees address are sharing information about the corporate benefits of family-friendly employee policies; children's health insurance plans; sufficient, affordable child care; investment of city and county funds in family support services; county definitions of abuse and neglect, and collaboration of local service agencies to serve children who have been identified as abused or neglected; and the local juvenile justice system.

Just as in working with legislators, it is important to state the issue being discussed and share the rationale for the position the company is being asked to take. Many corporate executives make decisions that are family friendly because it is "the right thing to do." However, individuals working in private-sector advocacy need to present rationales that make good business sense. It is much easier to influence corporate decision makers to make decisions that are good for children when the case can be made that the decision is also good for the corporation.

VOICES *of Families*

I would not have thought about approaching my employer with my concerns about child care until another parent asked me to sign a petition. I found myself talking to lots of employees and ended up talking with the president and vice-presidents of the company. It took over a year for them to make the decision to provide child care to employees, but without people like me willing to ask for what we needed, they might never have come to that decision.

Personal Advocacy

Not everyone is prepared to get involved in public policy or private-sector advocacy, but all early childhood educators can be involved in personal advocacy. Personal advocacy involves efforts to influence individuals or groups who make decisions that affect young children and their families.

Much of the time, this type of advocacy is informal and rather spontaneous. Personal advocacy can be as simple as talking with friends over lunch about an issue related to children. Beyond sharing information with friends, teachers can also share information with colleagues, administrators, and family members of students. Today people live very busy lives and find it difficult to keep up with laws and policies being considered. Casual conversations make people aware of bills or policies being considered, and many people will write a letter or make a telephone call if asked to.

Unlike public policy or private-sector advocacy, personal advocacy includes efforts to help people better understand how children learn and what teaching practices best support children's development. In this way, personal advocacy may include working with administrators. Administrators over early childhood programs do not always come to their positions with knowledge of child growth and development principles. When early childhood educators share their knowledge and their concerns about inappropriate programs in honest, open ways, administrators are likely to listen.

Personal advocacy may include working with colleagues. Teachers who are teaching young children have not always been trained as early childhood educators. For many reasons, teachers who have elementary certification take positions in preschool or primary grades. They may be well intentioned, warm, and caring. But if they have not taken courses specifically focused on young children, the way they interact with children, the expectations they have, and even their teaching strategies may be inappropriate for young children. Personal advocacy efforts may help change these inappropriate practices.

When organized, personal advocates can change actions of communities. Neighborhoods can be influenced to provide safer playground space for children. A city council can be encouraged to provide more space for children's recreation. Community-based and faith-based organizations can be swayed in their plans for providing child care or after-school programs for young children. Even colleges and universities can be convinced to offer more early childhood education courses.

Important Issues for Advocates to Remember

Taking on the role of advocate requires a certain amount of passion for the issue. This passion is good motivation for assuming the responsibility of advocacy, but advocates need to remember to back up their passion with reasoned debate. Even controversial issues should be discussed calmly, and people holding opposing positions must be respected. Advocates must be patient with people they encounter and with the process itself. No matter what the level of advocacy, virtually all advocacy efforts take time. People do not change quickly; nor do legislatures, school boards, city councils, business boards, or community organizations.

 Summary

Young children cannot act as advocates for policies and laws that affect them, so they depend on early childhood educators and their families to do this for them. True early childhood advocates speak out when they can and as often as they can, and are patient as they work to influence decisions that support young children and their families. Teachers should carefully consider the different advocacy roles and begin implementing advocacy efforts within their comfort level.

Reflections

1. Consider the list of issues related to young children and their families in Box 12.1. Think about laws that would improve the lives of young children.

Field Experiences

1. Visit the meeting of a local school board. Take notes on their decision-making process and the reactions they have to parents or teachers that address them.
2. Schedule a meeting with a local, state, or national legislator or a member of the legislator's staff, and ask about his or her position on a particular piece of legislation that affects young children.

Other Activities

1. Go to www.naeyc.org and locate the joint position statement of the National Association for the Education of Young Children (NAEYC) and the National Association of Early Childhood Specialists in State Departments of Education (NAECS/SDE) called "Early Learning Standards: Creating the Conditions for Success." Work in small groups to brainstorm ways this position statement could be used in advocacy efforts, then share with the entire group.
2. Go to http://www.cdfactioncouncil.org/ and sign up for the weekly legislative updates from the

Children's Defense Fund. Monitor the updates and be prepared to discuss legislative issues related to young children and their families.
3. Go to http://www.cwla.org/advocacy/advocacy resourcetips.htm and read the tips for advocates published by the Child Welfare League of America.
4. Do an Internet search to find the names of your state and national senators and representatives. Make a note regarding addresses, telephone numbers, fax numbers, and email addresses.
5. Do some research about currently pending bills related to young children or their families. Write to an appropriate legislator, asking about his or her position on this bill.

 Further Readings

Robinson, A., & Stark, D. R. (2002). *Advocates in Action: Making a difference for young children.* Washington, DC: National Association for the Education of Young Children.

This monograph defines three levels of advocacy—public policy, private-sector, and personal advocacy—and makes practical suggestions for influencing other people for the benefit of young children and their families.

 Websites to Explore

- Children's Defense Fund
  25 E Street NW
  Washington, DC 20001
  202-628-8787
  http://www.childrensdefense.org/
  The Children's Defense Fund began in 1973 and is a private, nonprofit organization supported by foundations, corporation grants, and individual donations. The mission of the Children's Defense Fund is to Leave No Child Behind® and to ensure every child a Healthy Start, a Head Start, a Fair Start, a Safe Start, and a Moral Start in life and successful passage to adulthood with the help of caring families and communities.

■ Kids Count

http://www.aecf.org/kidscount/

KIDS COUNT, a project of the Annie E. Casey Foundation, is a national and state-by-state effort to track the status of children in the United States. By providing policymakers and citizens with benchmarks of child well-being, KIDS COUNT seeks to enrich local, state, and national discussions concerning ways to secure better futures for all children.

■ Stand for Children

1420 Columbia Road, NW 3rd Floor

Washington, DC 20009

1-800-663-4032

http://www.stand.org/

Stand for Children is America's only nationwide grassroots voice for children. Members take action at the national, state, community, and neighborhood levels on issues from early childhood education and the schools to after-school programs and health services.

Appendix

Annotated Bibliography of Children's Books
(Different Cultures and Family Types)

Ammon, R. (2000). *An Amish year*. New York: Atheneum.

This book is just what the title claims, the story of a traditional Amish family's lives over an entire year.

Bercaw, E. C. (2000). *Halmoni's day*. New York: Puffin.

This is the story of Jennifer's grandmother, who travels all the way from Korea to attend Grandparents' Day at Jennifer's school.

Bunting, E. (1990). *The Wednesday surprise*. Glenview, IL: Scott Foresman.

A daughter and her grandmother work on a special birthday present for the girl's father. Having been taught to read by her granddaughter, the grandmother reads aloud for her son.

Bunting, E. (1993). *Fly away home*. Boston: Clarion Books.

Andrew and his father are homeless, living in an airport. The story shares how they try to blend in to their surroundings, but the real story is about the love between a father and son.

Bunting, E. (1997). *A day's work*. Boston: Houghton Mifflin.

This is a touching story of a family's immigration and their adjustment to life in America, with the grandson acting as translator for his grandfather, and the grandfather teaching his grandson important lessons of life.

Bunting, E. (1999). *A picnic in October*. San Diego: Harcourt.

Tony does not understand why his family always goes to the Statue of Liberty once a year and takes a picnic lunch and a birthday cake. On one of these trips, he finally begins to understand what the statue means to immigrant families like his.

Carling, A. L. (1998). *Mama and papa have a store*. New York: Dial.

This book describes one day in the life of a Chinese girl who lives above her parents' store in Guatemala City.

Cha, D. (1998). *Dia's story cloth*. New York: Lee & Low Books.

Basing her story on a Hmong story cloth, Cha tells the story of her family's escape from China, the time they spent in Laos and Thailand, and their immigration to the United States.

Choi, S. N. (1993). *Halmoni and the picnic*. Boston: Houghton Mifflin.

Halmoni immigrates to New York and has a difficult time adjusting to the new city until her granddaughter invites her to come to a school picnic in Central Park. The children love Halmoni's delicious Korean food and invite her to play their games and sing their songs.

Choi, S. N. (1997). *Yumni and Halmoni's trip*. Boston: Houghton Mifflin.

When Halmoni and her granddaughter go to Korea for a visit, Yumni is afraid her grandmother will not want to return to New York City. While focusing on Koreans and Korean-Americans, the grandmother/granddaughter relationship transcends cultural boundaries.

Collier, B. (2000). *Uptown*. New York: Holt.

Collier created beautiful illustrations with watercolor and collage to depict the high points of the Harlem neighborhood: the Apollo Theater, brownstone row houses, and local chicken and waffle shops. A young boy leads the tour of the neighborhood.

Cooper, M. (1998). *Gettin' through Thursday.* New York: Lee & Low Books.

Andre and his single mother have to be creative because the celebration for his good grades falls on Thursday, the day before his mother gets paid and the day they rarely have money.

Cowley, J. (2002). *Big tortilla moon.* Honesdale, PA: Boyd Mills Press.

Marta has a bad day at school, but when she comes home, her grandmother bakes tortillas and tells her a traditional Native American tale about how to deal with problems.

dePaola, T. (2000). *Nana upstairs, nana downstairs.* New York: Puffin.

Nana Upstairs was Tomie's great grandmother, and Nana Downstairs was his grandmother. When Nana Upstairs dies Tomie sees a shooting star in the sky that his mother explains was a kiss from Nana Upstairs. The same thing happens years later when Nana Downstairs dies.

dePaola, T. (1991). *Now one foot, now the other.* New York: Putnam.

When his grandfather has a stroke, Bobby helps him relearn many of the things that the grandfather taught Bobby when he was a toddler.

Falwell, C. (1995). *Feast for 10.* Boston: Houghton Mifflin.

Told in rhyme, this counting book shows an African American family shopping for groceries (one shopping cart), cooking dinner, then eating together ("ten hungry folks").

Friedman, I. R. (1993). *How my parents learned to eat.* Boston: Houghton Mifflin.

A biracial child tells the story of how her Japanese mother and American father met, got to know one another, and married.

Garland, S. (1998). *My father's boat.* New York: Scholastic Press.

Garland tells the story of a father who takes his son fishing in the Pacific Ocean, just off the coast of California. During their fishing trip, the father talks about their Vietnamese heritage, culture, and values.

Garland, S. (1998). *The lotus seed.* New York: Voyager Books.

A Vietnamese immigrant has carried a lotus seed taken from the Imperial Garden with her since childhood. Her grandson finds the seed, then proceeds to lose it. As she mourns the loss of her cherished seed, it blooms and she realizes that she will now have precious seeds to pass on to her grandchildren.

Garza, C. L. (2000). *In my family/En mi familia.* San Francisco: Childrens Book Press.

Using her own paintings and brief bilingual text, Garza shares her Hispanic background, from everyday events to special celebrations.

Hazen, B. S. (1983). *Tight times.* New York: Picture Puffins.

This story of a family experiencing financial difficulty is quite touching. The son wants a pet. The parents cannot afford it. The conclusion shows the child's ingenuity and the strong love this family has for each other.

Hoberman, M. A. (2001). *Mothers, fathers, sisters, and brothers: A collection of family poems.* New York: Little, Brown & Co.

This collection of poems illustrates a variety of family situations. All children will relate to these poems in one way or another.

Hoberman, M. A. (2001). *A house is a house for me.* Glenview, IL: Scott Foresman.

Supported by a text filled with rhyme and rhythm, this books depicts all kinds of houses, for people and animals alike.

Katz, K. (1999). *The colors of us.* New York: Henry Holt.

This story follows Lena and her mother as they observe how differences in skin color on people matches the color of foods and things found in nature.

Kurtz, J. (2000). *Faraway home.* New York: Gulliver.

Desta does not want her father to go back to Ethiopia. He is only going to visit his family, but she is afraid he will decide to stay there and not come back to his family in the United States.

Lin, G. (1999). *The ugly vegetables.* Watertown, MA: Charlesbridge.

A little girl dislikes her family's garden. Unlike the neighborhood flower gardens, their garden is full of what look like weeds. At harvest time, her mother cooks a wonderful soup from the *sheau hwang gua, torng hau,* and other Chinese vegetables, and the neighbors come to investigate the wonderful smells.

McGovern, A. (1999). *The lady in the box.* Hollidaysburg, PA: Turtle Books.

Two children take food and warm clothes to a homeless woman. When their mother finds out why food is missing from the house, they all go together to meet the homeless person. This prompts the family's work in a shelter.

Mora, P. (1997). *A birthday basket for Tia.* New York: Aladdin Library.

Based on her own experiences in Hispanic communities in El Paso, Texas, Mora tells the story of a family preparing a surprise party for a great aunt's ninetieth birthday. The food, music, and other traditions of Hispanic families is well depicted.

Morris, A. (2000). *Families.* New York: Harper-Collins.

The opening words, "Everyone, everywhere, is part of a family," are illustrated with photographs of families from Ethiopia, Canada, Vietnam, and the United States. The remainder of the book shares all kinds of families, showing how we are all alike and how we are different.

Morris, A. (1993). *Bread, bread, bread.* Glenview, IL: Scott Foresman.

Bread comes in different shapes, sizes, textures, and colors, as it varies from culture to culture. Morris's photographs of bread from around the world depict several cultures.

Morris, A. (1993). *Hats, hats, hats.* New York: Mulberry Books.

Morris's beautiful photographs show hats. from cultures around the world.

Morris, A. (1992). *Houses and homes.* New York: Lothrop, Lee & Sheppard.

The color photographs in this book offer a wide view of houses around the world. Different types of building materials, various sizes, and diverse types of homes are noted.

Newman, L. (2000). *Heather has two mommies.* Los Angeles: Alyson Publications.

Heather, who has two lesbian mothers, discovers at preschool that families are all different. The teacher encourages all the children to draw pictures of their families, sharing that all families are special and the important thing about families is that they love each other.

Polacco, P. (2001). *The keeping quilt.* New York: Aladdin Paperbacks.

Patricia Polacco's great-grandmother created a quilt from the clothing of relatives, and the quilt has been passed down to the family's fourth generation.

Polacco, P. (1998). *Chicken Sunday.* New York: Paper Star.

Patricia and two childhood friends convince the owner of a hat shop to let them sell eggs they've decorated as Pysanky eggs. They need the money to buy a hat for the boys' grandmother. Details of the lives of Russian immigrants and African Americans in the 1940s enhance the book's story line.

Polacco, P. (1994). *Just plain fancy.* New York: Picture Yearling.

Traditions of Amish families provide the background for the story of two Amish girls finding a strange-looking egg. They put it beside some chicken eggs. In time, this egg turns into a beautiful peacock, now living in a community where plain is valued.

Polacco, P. (1994). *Mrs. Katz & Tush.* New York: Picture Yearling.

This books tells the story of a budding friendship between a young African American boy and an elderly Russian Jewish immigrant woman.

Rylant, C. (1993). *When I was young in the mountains.* New York: E. P. Dutton.

Rylant bases this story on her own life, growing up with her grandparents in the Appalachian mountains where life is simple and family is important.

Say, A. (1991). *Tree of cranes.* Boston: Houghton Mifflin.

This is the story of a mother introducing her son to the holiday of Christmas she celebrated as a child in America.

Say, A. (1993). *Grandfather's journey.* Boston: Houghton Mifflin.

Say tells the story of his grandfather's immigration from Japan to the United States, his longing to return to the city of his birth, and that journey.

Senisi, E. B. (2001). *Brothers & sisters.* New York: Scholastic.

With little text except for captions for the culturally sensitive photographs, this book's unifying theme comes from the photos themselves. Each photograph celebrates the sibling relationship.

Simon, N. (1999). *All kinds of children.* Morton Grove, IL: Albert Whitman.

Watercolor illustrations lead the reader through a discussion of things children around the world have in common: food, clothing, love, an opportunity to play, and even a bellybutton.

Smith, C. L. (1999). *Jingle dancer.* New York: HarperCollins.

In a nonstereotypical portrayal of Native American life, Jenna is supported by friends and family as she gets ready for the big dance at an upcoming powwow. The focus of the story is Jenna's love for jingle dancing and preparing her jingle dress.

Soto, G. (1993). *Too many tamales.* New York: Putnam.

Gary Soto shares the Christmas tradition of many Hispanic families of making and eating tamales. Maria's mother is teaching her how to make tamales for the family.

Strickland, D., and Strickland, E. (1996). *Families: Poems celebrating the African American experience.* Honesdale, CA: Boyd Mills Press.

This is a collection of twenty-three poems about African American families, including "Thursday Evening Bedtime," "Aunt Sue's Stories," and "Families, Families."

Upitis, A. (2000). *Century farm: One hundred years on a family farm.* Honesdale, CA: Boyd Mills Press.

Photographs of one farm—and the family who works the farm—support the story of a Wisconsin farm. The story begins 100 years ago and ends in the present day.

Watts, J. H. (2000). *Keepers.* New York: Lee & Low Books.

Kenyon has saved money to buy a present for his grandmother. When he spends that money on a baseball glove, he has to come up with another present for his grandmother, one that doesn't cost any money. In trying to figure out what to give her, he gets to know his grandmother even better.

Wilhoite, W. (1991). *Daddy's roommate.* Los Angeles: Alyson Books.

Beginning with his parents' divorce, the book tells the story of a young boy whose father introduces him to a special friend who likes him and will help him feel safe and loved. The family activities shown occurring in the gay home are typical family activities.

Williams, V. B. (1984). *A chair for my mother.* Glenview, IL: Scott Foresman.

After all their furniture is destroyed in a fire, a little girl, her waitress mother, and her grandmother all save coins in a jar. They save enough money to buy a big, comfortable chair for their living room.

Yolen, J. (1987). *Owl moon.* New York: Philomel Books.

This book tells the story of a special time shared by a father and his daughter when they go owling in the woods late at night. *Owl Moon* won the 1988 Caldecott Award.

References

American Academy of Child and Adolescent Psychiatry. (1999a). *Facts on families: #15 The adopted child.* Retrieved June 2, 2002, from http:// www.aacap.org/web/aacap/ publications/factsfam/adopted.htm.

American Academy of Child and Adolescent Psychiatry. (1999b). *Facts on families: #27 Stepfamily problems.* Retrieved June 2, 2002, from http://www.aacap. org/web/ aacap/publications/factsfam/ stepfmly.htm.

American Academy of Child and Adolescent Psychiatry. (2000). *Facts on families: #77 Grandparents raising grandchildren.* Retrieved June 2, 2002, from http://www. aacap.org/web/aacap/publications/ factsfam/77.htm.

American Academy of Child and Adolescent Psychiatry. (2002). *Facts on families: #64 Foster care.* Retrieved June 2, 2002, from http://www.aacap.org/web/aacap/ publications/factsfam/64.htm.

Ballen, J., & Moles, O. (1994). *Strong families, strong schools.* Washington, DC: United States Department of Education.

Bauch, P. A. (2001). School-community partnerships in rural schools: Leadership, renewal, and a sense of place. *Peabody Journal of Education, 76* (2), 204–221

Baumann, J. F., & Thomas, D. (1998). "If you can pass Momma's tests, then she knows you're getting your education": A case study of support for literacy learning within an African American family. *Reading Teacher, 51,* 108–120.

Berger, E. H. (1991). Parent involvement: Yesterday and today. *Elementary School Journal, 91*(3), 209–219.

Bess, S. (1994). *Nobody don't love nobody: Lessons on love from the school with no name.* Placerville, CA: Goldleaf Press.

Bloome, D., Katz, L., Wilson-Keenan, J., & Solsken, J. (2000). Interpellations of family/community and classroom literacy practices. *Journal of Educational Research, 93,* 155–164.

Boone, K. and Barclay, E. (1995). *Building a three-way partnership: The leader's role in linking school, parents, and community.* New York: Scholastic.

Bracey, G. W. (2001). School involvement and the working poor. *Phi Delta Kappan, 82,* 95–96.

Brandt, R. (1989). On parents and schools: A conversation with Joyce Epstein. *Educational Leadership, 47,* 24–27.

Bredekamp, S., & Copple, C. (Eds.). (1997). *Developmentally appropriate practice in early childhood programs,* Rev. ed. Washington, DC: National Association for the Education of Young Children.

Bruns, D. A., & Corso, R. M. (2001). *Working with culturally & linguistically diverse families.* ERIC Reproduction Document Number 455972.

Buell, M. J., Hallam, R.A., & Beck, H. L. (2001). Early Head Start and child care partnerships: Working together to serve infants, toddlers, and their families. *Young Children, 56,* 7–12.

Bullough, R. V., Jr. (2001). *Uncertain lives: Children of promise, teachers of hope.* New York: Teachers College Press.

Cable News Network. (1998, May 28). Decline of traditional family slows in 90s. Retrieved June 25, 2002, from http://www.cnn.com/ US/9805/28/family.figures/.

Calkins, L. McC., & Bellino, L. (1998). *Raising lifelong learners: A parents' guide.* Cambridge, MA: Perseus Press.

Carle, E. (1998). *Pancakes, pancakes.* New York: Aladdin Paperbacks.

Cesarone, B. (2000). Parent-teacher conference. *Childhood Education, 76,* 180–181.

Chaboudy, R., Jameson, P., & Huber, J. (2001). Connecting families and schools through technology. *Book Report, 20,* 52–58.

Chavkin, N. F., & Gonzalez, D. L. 1995. *Forging partnerships between Mexican American parents and the schools*. ERIC Reproduction Document Number 388489.

Chavkin, N. F., & Gonzalez, D. L. (2000). Forging partnerships between Mexican American parents and the schools. ERIC Reproduction Document Number ED388489.

Children's Defense Fund. (2001). *The state of America's children, 2001*. Washington, DC: Author.

Christensen, B. (1996). *Building parent partnerships*. Washington, DC: National Education Association.

Clark, A. (1999). *Parent-teacher conferences: Suggestions for parents*. ERIC Reproduction Service Number 433965.

Cline, Z. (2001). Reading parties: Helping families share the joy of literacy. *Reading Teacher, 55*, 236–237.

Coleman, M. (1991). *Planning for parent participation in schools for young children*. ERIC Reproduction Document Number 3422463.

Coleman, M. (1997). Families and schools: In search of common ground. *Young Children, 52*, 14–21.

Cullinan, B. E. (2000). *Read to me: Raising kids who love to read*. New York: Scholastic.

Desimone, L., Finn-Stevenson, M., & Henrich, C. (2000). Whole school reform in a low income African American community. *Urban Education, 35*, 269–324.

Diffily, D. (2000). *Early childhood educators' beliefs and practices about family involvement*. Unpublished raw data.

Diffily, D. (2001). Family meetings: Building relationships between the teacher and families. *Dimensions of Early Childhood, 29*, 5–10.

Diffily, D., & Morrison, K. (Eds.). (1997). *Family-friendly communication in early childhood programs*. Washington, DC: National Association for the Education of Young Children.

Dresser, N. (1996). *Multicultural manners: New rules of etiquette for a changing society*. New York: John Wiley and Sons.

Dyer, W. W. (2001). *What do you really want for your children?* New York: Avon Books.

Egley, E. H., & Egley, R. J. (2000). Teaching principals, parents, and colleagues about developmentally appropriate practice. *Young Children, 55*, 48–51.

Eldridge, D. (2001). Parent involvement: It's worth the effort. *Young Children, 56*, 65–69.

Epstein, J. L. (1991). Paths to partnership: What we can learn from federal, state, district, and school initiatives. *Phi Delta Kappan, 72*, 344–349.

Epstein, J. L. (1996). Advances in family, community, and school partnerships. *Community Education Journal, 23*, 10–15.

Epstein, J. L. (2001). *School, family, and community partnerships: Preparing educators and improving schools*. Boulder, CO: Westview Press.

Epstein, J. L., Sanders, M. G., Simon, B. S., Salinas, K. C., Johnson, N. R., & Van Voorhis, F. L. (2003). *School, family and community partnerships: Your handbook for action*, 2nd ed. Los Angeles: Corwin Press.

ERIC Clearing House on Urban Education. (2001). *Latinos in school: Some facts and findings*. ERIC Reproduction Document Number 449288.

Espinosa, L. M. (1995). *Hispanic parent involvement in early childhood programs*. ERIC Reproduction Document Number 382412.

Faires, J., Nichols, W. D., & Rickelman, R. J. (2000). Effects of parental involvement in developing competent readers in first grade. *Reading Psychology, 21*(3), 195–216.

Fan, X., & Chen, M. J. (1999). Academic achievement of rural school students: A multi-year comparison with their peers in suburban and urban schools. *Journal of Research in Rural Education, 15*(1), 31–46.

Faucette, E. (2001). Are you missing the most important ingredient? A recipe for increasing student achievement. *MultiMedia Schools, 7*, 56–58, 60–61.

Fields, J. (2001). *Living arrangements of children: Fall 1996*. Washington, DC: U.S. Department of Commerce, U.S. Census Bureau, Current Population Reports, P70–74.

File, N. (2001). Family-professional partnerships: Practice that matches philosophy. *Young Children, 56*, 70–74.

Fuller, M. L. (1993). Today's demographics don't leave it to beaver. *Education Digest, 58,* 54–57.

Galinsky, E. (1990). Why are some parent-teacher relationships clouded with difficulties? *Young Children, 45,* 38–39.

Galinsky, E., & David, J. (1991). *The preschool years: Family strategies that work—From experts and parents.* New York: Ballantine.

Gestwicki, C. (2000). *Home, school, and community relations,* 4th ed. Albany, NY: Delmar.

Gorter-Reu, M. S., & Anderson, J. M. (1998). Home kits, home visits, and more! *Young Children, 53,* 71–74.

Hale-Benson, J. (1986). *Black children: Their roots, culture, and learning styles.* Baltimore, MD: Johns Hopkins University Press.

Harwayne, Shelley. (1999). *Going public.* Portsmouth, NH: Heinemann.

Henderson, A. T. (1987). *The evidence continues to grow.* Columbia, MD: National Committee for Citizens in Education.

Henderson, A., & Berla, N. (1981). *The evidence grows.* Washington, DC: National Committee for Citizens in Education.

Henderson, A., & Berla, N. (1995). *A new generation of evidence: The family is critical to student achievement.* Washington, DC: Center for Law and Education.

Hollingsworth, H. L. (2001). We need to talk: Communication strategies for effective collaboration. *Teaching Exceptional Children, 33,* 6–9.

Hurt, J. A. (2000). Create a parent place: Make the invitation for family involvement real. *Young Children, 55,* 88–92.

Hymes, J. L. (2002). *But why a co-op?* Retrieved October 28, 2002, from http://www.ccppns.org/notes.html.

Jones, R. (2001). Involving parents is a whole new game: Be sure you win. *Education Digest, 67,* 38–46.

Jongsma, K. (2001). Literacy links between home and school. *Reading Teacher, 55,* 58–61.

Jordan, C., Orozco, E., & Averett, A. (2002). *Emerging issues in school, family, & community connections, Annual synthesis, 2001.* ERIC Reproduction Document Number 464411.

Katz, L. G. (1996). *Preventing and resolving parent-teacher differences.* ERIC Reproduction Document Number 401048.

Kaufman, H. O. (2001). Skills for working with all families. *Young Children, 56,* 81–83.

Koch, P. K., & McDonough, M. (1999). Improving parent-teacher conferences through collaborative conversations. *Young Children, 54,* 11–15.

Kotlowitz, A. (1992). *There are no children here: The story of two boys growing up in the other America.* New York: Random House.

Kozol, J. (1992). *Savage inequalities: Children in America's schools.* New York: HarperCollins.

Ladson-Billings, G. (1997). *Dreamkeepers: Successful teachers of African-American teachers.* San Francisco: Jossey-Bass.

Lazar, A., & Slostad, F. (1999). How to overcome obstacles to parent-teacher partnerships. *Clearing House 72,* 206–210.

Lee, G. L., & Manning, M. L. (2001). Treat Asian parents and families right. *Education Digest, 67,* 39–46.

Little Soldier, L. (1997). Is there an "Indian" in your classroom? Working successfully with urban Native Americans. *Phi Delta Kappan, 78,* 650–653.

Love, F. E. (1996). Communicating with parents: What beginning teachers can do. *College Student Journal, 30,* 440–444.

Lynch, E. W., & Hanson, M. J. (Eds.). (1997). *Developing cross-cultural competence: A guide for working with children and their families,* 2nd ed. Baltimore: Paul H. Brookes.

Manning, D., & Schindler, P. J. (1997). Communicating with parents when their children have difficulties. *Young Children, 52,* 27–33.

Mapp, K. (1997). Making family-school connections work. *Education Digest, 63,* 36–40.

Marshall, N. L., Noonan, A. E., McCartney, K., Marx, F., & Keefe, N. (2001). It takes an urban village. *Journal of Family Issues, 22,* 163–183.

Martin, E. J., & Hagan-Burke, S. (2002). Establishing a home-school connection: Strengthening the partnership between families and schools. *Preventing School Failure, 46,* 62–66.

Martinez, Y. G., & Velazquez, J. A. (2000). *Involving migrant families in education.* ERIC Reproduction Document Number 448010.

McBride, S. L. (1999). Family-centered practices, research in review. *Young Children, 54,* 62–68.

McWilliam, R. A., & Maxwell, R. L. (1999). Beyond "involvement": Are elementary schools ready to be family-centered? *School Psychology Review, 28,* 378–388.

National Association for the Education of Young Children. (1998). *Accreditation Criteria and Procedures of the National Association for the Education of Young Children.* Washington, DC: Author.

National Law Center on Homelessness and Poverty. (1999). *Out of sight—Out of mind? A report on anti-homeless laws, litigation, and alternatives in 50 United States cities.* Washington, DC: Author.

National PTA (2002). *National standards for parent/family involvement.* Retrieved May 16, 2002, from http://www.pta.org/programs/pfistand.htm#.

Nelsen, J., Duffy, R., & Erwin, C. (1998). *Positive discipline for preschoolers: For their early years—Raising children who are responsible, respectful, and resourceful.* Rocklin, CA: Prima Publishing.

Nistler, R. J., & Maiers, A. (1999). Exploring home-school connections: A family literacy perspective on improving urban schools. *Education and Urban Society, 32,* 3–17.

Nord, C. W. (1998). *Father involvement in schools.* ERIC Digest. ERIC Reproduction Document Number 419632.

Okagaki, L., & Diamond, K. E. (2000). Responding to cultural and linguistic differences in the beliefs and practices of families with young children. *Young Children, 55,* 74–80.

Payne, R. 1995. *Poverty: A framework for understanding and working with students and adults from poverty.* Baytown, TX: RFT Publishing.

Powell, D. (1989). *Families and early childhood programs.* Washington, DC: National Association for the Education of Young Children.

Proud Parenting. (2002.) *Over 3 million children live with gay parents.* Retrieved October 20, 2002 from http://www.proudparenting. com/page.cfm?sectionid=4.

Puckett, M. P., & Diffily, D. (1999). *Teaching young children: An introduction to the early childhood profession.* Fort Worth, TX: Harcourt Brace.

Quigley, D. D. (2000). *Parents and Teachers Working Together To Support Third Grade Achievement: Parents as Learning Partners (PLP) Findings.* ERIC Reproduction Document Number ED440787

Quiroz, B., Greenfield, P. M., & Altchech, M. (1999). Bridging cultures with a parent-teacher conference. *Educational Leadership 56,* 68–70.

Rich, D. (1998). *Megaskills: Building children's achievement for the information age.* New York: Mariner Books.

Riggs, S., & Dunn, R. (1996). *Hispanic American students and learning styles.* ERIC Reproduction Document Number 393607.

Rimm-Kaufman, S. E., & Pianta, R. C. (1999). Patterns of family-school contact in preschool and kindergarten. *School Psychology Review, 28,* 426–439.

Robinson, A., & Stark, D. R. (2002). *Advocates in action: Making a difference for young children.* Washington, DC: National Association for the Education of Young Children.

Rockwell, R. E., Andre, L. C., & Hawley, M. K. (1995). *Parents and teachers as partners: Issues and challenges.* Fort Worth: Harcourt Brace.

Roe, K. M., & Minkler, M. (1998/99). Grandparents raising grandchildren: Challenges and responses. *Generations, 22,* 25–33.

Rose, M. C. (1998). Handle with care: The difficult parent-teacher conference. *Instructor 108,* 92–93, 101.

Saluter, A. (1996). *Marital status and living arrangements: Current population reports series.* Washington, DC: National Center for Health Statistics.

Sanders, M. G., Epstein, J. L., & Connors-Tadros, L. (1999). *Family Partnerships with High Schools: The Parents' Perspective. Report No. 32.* ERIC Reproduction Document Number 428148

Schlossman, S. L. (1976). Before Head Start: Notes toward a history of parent education in

America, 1897–1929. *Harvard Educational Review, 46,* 436–467.

Schwartz, W. (1995). *School programs and practices for homeless students.* (Report No. EDO-UD-95-2). Washington, DC: Office of Educational Research and Improvement, U.S. Department of Education. (ERIC Document Reproduction Service Digest No. 105.)

Schwartz, W. (1999a). *Family diversity in urban schools.* ERIC Digest. ERIC Reproduction Document Number 434188.

Schwartz, W. (1999b). *School support for foster families.* ERIC Digest. ERIC Reproduction Document Number 434189.

Schwartz, W. (1999c). *Arab American students in public schools.* ERIC Reproduction Document Number 429144.

Schweinhart, L. J., & Weikart, D. P. (1986). Early childhood development programs: A public investment opportunity. *Educational Leadership, 44*(3), 4–12 .

Southworth, S. A. (2000). Talk time: Communicate effectively with parents, and maximize students' school success. *Instructor 110,* 31–32.

Stacey, J., & Biblarz, T. J. 2001. (How) Does the sexual orientation of parents matter? *American Sociological Review, 66,* 159–183.

Stevenson, D. L., & Baker, D. P. (1987). The family-school relation and the child's school performance. *Child Development, 58,* 1348–1358

Stipek, D., & Seal, K. (2001). *Motivated minds: Raising children to love learning.* Berkeley, CA: Owl Press.

Sturdler, R. (1993). Doesn't he have beautiful blue eyes? Tips for a successful parent-teacher conference. *Preventing School Failure 37,* 11–13.

Sturm, C. (1997). Creating parent-teacher dialogue: Intercultural communication in child care. *Young Children, 52,* 34–38.

Swap, S. M. (1993). *Developing home-school partnerships: From concepts to practice.* New York: Teachers College Press.

Swick, K. J. (1992). *Teacher-parent partnerships.* ERIC Reproduction Document Number 351149.

Swick, K. (1996). Building healthy families: Early childhood educators can make a difference. *Journal of Instructional Psychology, 23,* 75–82.

Swick, K. J., & Graves, S. B. (1993). *Empowering at-risk families during the early childhood years.* Washington, DC: National Education Association.

Szemcsak, D. D., & West, O. J. (1996). The whole town is talking about it . . . Math month, that is. *Teaching Children Mathematics, 3,* 179–173.

Tatum, B. D. (1997). *Why are all the black kids sitting together in the cafeteria? and other conversations about race.* New York: Basic Books.

Trelease, J. (2001). *The read-aloud handbook,* 5th ed. New York: Penguin.

Turbiville, V. P., Umbarger, G. T., & Guthrie, A. C. (2000). Fathers' involvement in programs for young children. *Young Children, 55,* 74–79.

United States Census Bureau (2001). *American factfinder of 2000 census.* Retrieved June 1, 2002 from http://factfinder.census.gov/.

Walker-Dalhouse, D., & Dalhouse, A. D. (2001). Parent-school relations: Communicating more effectively with African American parents. *Young Children, 56,* 75–80.

Webb, N. C. (1997). Working with parents from cradle to preschool: A university collaborates with an urban public school. *Young Children, 52,* 15–19.

Weissbourd, B. (Ed.). (1987). *Brief history of programs in America's family supported programs: The origins and development of a movement.* New Haven, CT: Yale University Press.

Whipple, G. M. (1929). *Twenty-eighth yearbook of the National Society for the Study of Education: Preschool and parent education.* Bloomington, IL: Public School Publishing.

Zigler, E., & Muenchow, S. (1994). *Head Start: The inside story of America's most successful educational experiment.* New York: Basic Books.

Index